Also of interest

Ethical Principles for Social Policy
Edited by John Howie

Ethical Principles
and
Practice

Edited by John Howie

Southern Illinois University Press

Carbondale and Edwardsville

Copyright © 1987 by the Board of Trustees,
Southern Illinois University
All rights reserved
Printed in the United States of America
Designed by Dan Gunter
Production supervised by Natalia Nadraga
90 89 88 87   4 3 2 1

Library of Congress Cataloging-in-Publication Data

Ethical principles and practice.

Bibliography: p.
Includes index.
1. Ethics. 2. Social ethics. I. Howie, John.
BJ1012.E883   1987   170   86-33897
ISBN 0-8093-1410-X

The paper used in this publication meets the minimum
requirements of American National Standard for Information
Sciences–Permanence of Paper for Printed
Library Materials, ANSI Z39.48-1984. ⬯™

For Beverly

Contents

Contributors

Michael D. Bayles was Director of the Westminster Institute for Ethics and Human Values at Westminster College, London, Canada, before taking his present post as Professor of Philosophy, University of Florida, Gainesville. He is the author of *Principles of Legislation: The Uses of Political Authority* (1978), *Morality and Population Policy* (1980), *Professional Ethics* (1981), *Reproductive Ethics* (1984), and *Principles of Law* (1987). He is the editor of *Contemporary Utilitarianism* (1978), *Ethics and Population* (1976), and the coeditor of *Medical Treatment of the Dying: Moral Issues* (with Dallas M. High, 1978), *Right Conduct: Theories and Applications* (with Kenneth Henley, 1982), and *Justice, Rights and Tort Law* (with Bruce Chapman, 1983). More than seventy of his articles have been published in professional journals.

Abraham Edel, Research Professor of Philosophy at the University of Pennsylvania since 1974, served for more than forty years as an outstanding teacher at the City University of New York. Recipient of numerous academic and professional honors, Edel is the author or editor of a dozen books, including *The Theory and Practice of Philosophy* (1946), *Ethical Judgment: The Use of Science in Ethics* (1955), *Anthropology and Ethics* (with May Edel, 1959; rev. ed., 1970), *Science and the Structure of Ethics* (1961), *Method in Ethical Theory* (1963), *Analyzing Concepts in Social Science* (1979), *Exploring Fact and Value* (1980), *Aristotle and His Philosophy* (1982), and *Interpreting Education* (1985).

Warner A. Wick, late William Rainey Harper Professor, Department of Philosophy, University of Chicago, and editor of *Ethics*, is the author of *Metaphysics and the New Logic* (1942) and a group of penetrating articles on ethics and the philosophy of Kant, including "Truth's Debt to Freedom," "Kant's Moral Philosophy," "Generalization and The Basis of Ethics," "The Pursuit of Wisdom: Reflections on Some Recent Pursuers," and "Social Problems in Precept and Example." Active in university administration at Chicago, he served as Dean of Students in the Humanities, Associate Dean of the College, Dean of Students in the University, Master of the Humanities Collegiate Division, and Associate Dean of the Division of the Humanities.

John Lachs, Professor of Philosophy at Vanderbilt University since 1967, has distinguished himself as a teacher and scholar. He is the recipient of the Phi Beta Kappa Faculty Award, the E. Harris Harbison Award, the Chancellor's Cup, and the Madison Sarratt Prize for outstanding teaching. In addition to more than fifty articles in journals, Lachs is the editor of *Animal Faith and Spiritual Life: Unpublished and Uncollected Works of George Santayana* (1967), *Physical Order and Moral Liberty* (with Shirley Lachs, 1969), and *The Human Search* (with Charles E. Scott, 1981). He is the author of *Intermediate Man* (1981); a book of poems, *The Ties of Time* (1970), and a book of essays, *Mind and Philosophers* (1986).

James F. Childress, Edwin B. Kyle Professor of Religious Studies and Professor of Medical Education at the University of Virginia, is the author of *Civil Disobedience and Political Obligation: A Study in Christian Social Ethics* (1971), *Priorities in Biomedical Ethics* (1981), *Moral Responsibility in Conflicts: Essays on Nonviolence, War, and Conscience* (1982), *Who Shall Decide? Paternalism in Health Care* (1982), and co-author (with Tom L. Beauchamp) of *Principles of Biomedical Ethics* (2nd ed., 1983). In 1984–85 he was a Guggenheim Fellow and a Fellow at the Woodrow Wilson International Center for Scholars. He was vice chairman of the federal Task Force on Organ Transplantation and is a member of the Working Group on Human Gene Therapy of the Recombinant DNA Advisory Committee.

Carl Wellman, Professor of Philosophy at Washington University, St. Louis, since 1968, is the author of *The Language of Ethics* (1961), *Challenge and Response: Justification in Ethics* (1971), *Morals and Ethics* (1975), *Welfare Rights* (1982), *A Theory of Rights: Persons Under Laws, Institutions, and Morals* (1985), and the editor of *Equality and Freedom: Past, Present and Future* (1977). He has been awarded fellowships including a Sheldon Travelling Fellowship (1951–52), an American Council of Learned Societies Fellowship (1965–66), an NEH Senior Fellowship (1972–73), and a National Humanities Center Fellowship (1982–83). He serves on the editorial boards of *Ethics* and *Archiv für Rechts-und Sozialphilosophie* and in leadership posts with various philosophical organizations including the International Association for Philosophy of Law and Social Philosophy and the American Philosophical Association Committee on Philosophy and Law.

Acknowledgments

It is a pleasure to acknowledge openly assistance and encouragement. For typing and special care with corrections, thanks to Dawn Boone and Michelle Perino. For proofreading and discussion of some of the ideas, appreciation is expressed to Bruce Smith and Rick Luczak. For completing difficult bibliographical entries the effort and diligence of Blake Landor is gratefully acknowledged. Thanks to Michael D. Bayles and Peter Dalton for permission to publish, with slight revisions, "Moral Theory and Application." This essay is reprinted with permission from *Social Theory and Practice* 10, no. 1 (Spring 1984): 97–120, copyright © 1984 by *Social Theory and Practice*. Mrs. Warner (Peggy) Wick has given permission to publish her late husband's essay "The Good Person and The Good Society: Some Ideals, Foolish and Otherwise." It, together with the essays by Edel, Lachs, Childress, and Wellman, are all published here for the first time.

The Wayne Leys Memorial Lectureship Fund, under management of the Southern Illinois University Foundation, makes possible these special lectures by outstanding philosophers. This is the second group of six such lectures emphasizing the relation of ethical theory to practice and its relevance to contemporary moral issues. In reflecting this emphasis they constitute an appropriate living memorial to Wayne Leys, who served so ably our Department and the larger concerns of the philosophical profession.

John Howie

Introduction

For more than a decade the Wayne Leys Memorial Lectureship, under the management of the Southern Illinois University Foundation, and in cooperation with the Philosophy Department has made possible each year a lecture by an outstanding visiting philosopher. This collection is the second group of six such lectures, revised for publication, emphasizing the relation of ethical principles to contemporary moral problems.

The first three essays deal with the general problem of how ethical theory is related to practice or application. Michael D. Bayles suggests that several features of legal reasoning provide guidance in conceiving the relationship of theory to practice or application. Of these, "midlevel bridging principles" make application possible and, in being applied, are themselves, in turn, modified. Formulating these principles and weighing them together constitute the primary task of applied ethicists. Differences between utilitarians and Kantians, for example, arise because, although they agree on such midlevel principles as confidentiality and truth-telling, they assign these principles different values and this results in different suggested moral actions. Sharp theoretical differences are reduced at the stage of midlevel principles to borderline and hard cases. This approach has the effect of narrowing the areas of disagreement.

If ethical theory and practice are conceived as related in this manner, then one can expect applied ethics to provide a clarification of what is relevant to problems, a formulation and revision of midlevel principles, rules specifying directives for classes of actions, conceptual or institutional procedures for deciding particular actions or policies, a narrowing of the range of disagreement, and some effective modification of individual, organizational, and governmental decisions.

Abraham Edel takes a different view of ethical theory and application or practice. For him the situation is less one of applying theories than of using them in situations where they help. Ethical theories, in any case, require definitions, interpretations, and operational procedures. The theoretical concepts and operational procedures direct the moral reaction or moral intuition. They are aids in raising deliberative questions about the situations confronted. Applying ethics is a matter of insight and exploration, of broadening and refining. Theory is as much applied practice as practice is applied theory.

The implications of this approach include (1) ethical theories must surrender their universal pretensions, (2) a pluralistic approach must be employed, permitting different ethical theories to assist us in different situations, (3) ethical theory functions to clarify, diagnose, and structure the situation, and (4) such theory may often be altered through the situation or the moral response. The simple rule-application approach overlooks the complexity and indeterminacy of the world and makes creative responses impossible.

Warner A. Wick focuses on the more restricted topic of applied ideals ("idealism") and fanaticism. He asks: does the application of ideals invariably result in fanaticism or foolishness? Ideals are those values that we esteem beyond price and that unsophisticated morality takes for granted. Ideals cannot be appropriately considered by any calculus of utilities or preferences.

To show that commitment to ideals need not result in fanaticism he invites us to consider three ideals that avoid this charge. For him the ideal of equal justice under law is the basis for employing the coercive power of government to enforce the legal order. Doing something because it is right is different from doing something because it pays. And individuals can act for ethically significant reasons even when they are acting against their own wants and desires. The second ideal, that of good will toward others, means helping others by making available the means and opportunities for them to act or equipment for their achieving their goals. A third ideal that seems to underlie every genuine virtue is that of integrity. It is a duty to ourselves. We can improve others by improving ourselves even as we can improve ourselves by improving others.

These three summary categories (justice, self-regarding duties, and good will to others) taken together constitute the comprehensive ideal of an ethical community of the free enjoying mutually sustained levels of welfare. But commitment to these ideals does not open the way to fanaticism since these ideals are self-determined and require for their pursuit respect for the equal liberty of others. To ignore the interconnections of ideals, or to assume that coercive measures can be a means to attain a worthy ideal is to flirt with fanaticism. To embrace ideals that ignore human weakness is mere foolishness.

John Lachs, in "Public Benefit, Private Costs," insists that the task of philosophy is to show the interconnectedness of personal and social life and in ethics to regain the unity of intention, performance, and consequences so that freedom and responsibility are not separated. His focus is not on the question of whether theory can be applied to practice, but rather what are the specific obstacles that prevent or impede us in applying ethical principles in our contemporary society. On the surface it appears that the great wealth and stability of industrial society are developed through manipulation, passivity, psychic distance, powerlessness, and psychic impoverishment of its individual members. But this is not a complete account since the social benefits of mediated action are undeniable and enormous: better human health, longer life expectancy, and increased comforts of every sort. A balanced assessment of these costs and benefits can be provided by philosophy.

To minimize these costs and maximize the benefits, society can help individual participants in mediated social actions regain immediacy through direct encounter with other agents and processes, foster direct and indirect communication among the participants, and formulate stern rules of responsibility, linking the individual's contribution to the larger social actions and consequences. These activities will join freedom with responsibility and enable ethical principles to be applied at work, in the political arena, and in our private lives.

James F. Childress directs our attention in his essay to the problems associated with obtaining and distributing organs for transplantation. The major relevant ethical principles are respect for persons and their bodies, justice in the distribution of burdens and benefits, the involvement of the family in sharing, and the promotion of community through acts of generosity. Different ethical perspectives arise because these principles are weighed and applied in different ways. There may be several ethically acceptable actions even though there may be only one or perhaps a few ethically preferable actions. Both the acceptable and the preferable must be distinguished from the politically feasible.

On the one hand, by emphasizing individuals as familial decision-makers, by "required consent" for organ donations, and by "tacit consent," the number of organ donations may be increased. On the other, the sale of organs, tax credits, and family credit for organ donations seem to violate the basic ethical principles of justice, respect for persons, and generosity. There is less agreement concerning just or equitable distribution of available organs. Most would agree on some criteria of "medical utility." Such utility is gauged by the need for and the probability of benefiting from an organ transplant, although occasionally there is a conflict between urgency of need and probability of success. Does one choose the patient in most urgent need? Or, does one rather choose the patient with the highest probability of benefiting from the transplant? There is some disagreement over whether the medical criteria are to be understood in a strict or loose sense.

Far more disagreement centers on the use of criteria of "social utility." These criteria focus on the value of the salvageable patients. They include the age of the recipient, life-style of the recipient, and social network of support for the recipient. Generally speaking, if a younger recipient for the transplant is selected, the chances of success are increased. Similarly, if a recipient whose life-style is healthful is chosen, success is more likely. And, further, if the recipient of the transplant has a strongly supportive network of friends and relatives, the likelihood of success is enhanced.

Who should pay for transplants, individuals or governments? This is another troublesome question. The major argument that the government should pay is that it is unfair to ask people to donate organs if the organs are then going to be distributed on the basis of ability to pay rather than need, however urgent or efficaciousness.

Carl Wellman, in his essay, explores the problem of whether or not a utilitarian justification of terrorism can be provided if one takes human rights seriously. He thinks that such a justification can be provided under some very restricted circumstances. Having as its end coercion, terrorism seems to violate a person's moral rights to freedom, property, and security of person. A preponderant utilitarian justification would be required to show the rights protected by acts of terrorism outweigh those violated by such actions.

While granting that it is theoretically possible to provide such a justification, Wellman argues that the terrorist actions of antiabortionists, for example, cannot be justified because of the presuppositions of those defending the antiabortionist view and because such actions are an ineffective way to protect the lives of the unborn and result in indiscriminate destruction of untainted property of innocent persons.

Consider, for example, the right of property. This right consists in the duty of others not to destroy or damage one's property, and the moral claim of the property owner to require performance or remedy if property is threatened or damaged. Property is whatever the social rules of one's society gives one the freedom and control to possess, use, and dispose of. This moral right to property has a correlative duty that others comply with it. If they do not comply, moral sanctions may be imposed on those who violate the rule. The utility of acting in conformity with the property rule together with the utility of acts imposing moral sanctions on those who violate the rule comprise the ultimate ground of the moral duty not to damage or destroy property.

Why is it useful to comply with the property rule? Wellman offers several reasons: (1) violations of the property rule reduce the supply of goods available for human use, (2) compliance with the property rule preserves security of possession of the right-holder, (3) destroying or damaging property brings resentment and/or retaliation, (4) breaking the property rule often brings out precautionary measures that are unproductive uses of resources and services, and (5) damaging or destroying property may provoke preemptive strikes that result in additional destruction and harm to persons.

The advantages of imposing these moral sanctions are fewer wasted resources, less interference with human projects requiring property, and a decrease in social conflicts. In addition, and positively, moral sanctions have educational value and strengthen social solidarity.

The right of property, then, has a complex utilitarian basis that cannot be easily overridden by any other single utilitarian consideration. Anti-abortion terrorism has not provided a convincing justification grounded in human rights. And only a rights-based justification can provide a warrant for deeds that violate human rights to person and property.

Showing the relevance of ethical theory to practice and the bearing of ethical principles on contemporary moral issues, in keeping with Leys' emphasis, these essays direct attention to the perennial and present-day issues of abortion, fanaticism, terrorism, human rights, and the technological revolution with its attendant problems and consequences. The reader is invited to reflect upon bridging principles that reduce moral disagreements and help one to judge the cogency of moral arguments, to recognize that creative ethical responses are born of wedding theory with practice, to realize that devotion to ideals need be neither fanatical nor foolish, to admit that sweeping social and technological achievements undermine relationships essential for moral responsibility, and to explore the complex and troublesome relation of terrorism to human rights. An intelligent reader will surely benefit from reflecting upon these issues.

John Howie

*Ethical Principles
and
Practice*

1

Moral Theory and Application
Michael D. Bayles

For many observers applied ethics as it has emerged in the last decade or
so has not lived up to its original promise. Some have challenged not so
much the need for ethics as the content of the ethical views that are developing.[1] However, a more fundamental (and therefore more bother-
some) criticism has come from those outside the field who have ques-
tioned whether there is any need for applied ethics, whether applied
ethics can do anything useful. Regardless of the reason for this criticism, be it disillusionment or something else altogether, it is legitimate
to ask what applied ethics can reasonably be expected to do. Unfortunately, the field has never given a perspicuous and perspicacious answer
to this question.

A second criticism has come from within the field. This internal criticism pertains to the methodology allegedly used by many applied ethicists. The thrust of the criticism is that much of applied ethics has been
too abstract, rigid, and divorced from the concrete problems faced by
practitioners in fields considered by applied ethics, such as population,
biomedicine, and other professions. A different methodology seeking
solutions to problems in particular contexts is advocated. This criticism
is not unrelated to the first; indeed, it may be a refinement of it. The
external criticism claims that applied ethics does not contribute to
the resolution of problems faced by people in concrete situations, and
the internal criticism claims that this has resulted from the employment
of an inappropriate methodology.

To consider these criticisms, it is necessary to investigate in detail the

Reprinted with permission from *Social Theory and Practice* 10, no. 1 (Spring 1984):
97–120. Copyright © 1984 by *Social Theory and Practice*.

relationship between moral theory and application.[2] Only when one has a reasonably clear and sound statement of the relationship between theory and application can one determine what can legitimately be expected from applied ethics.

Two Methodological Extremes

The internal critics attack an alleged commonly practiced method that some call deductivism. A few have suggested a more concrete situational approach that can be called pragmatic eclecticism. The deductivist approach to the application of moral theory must be distinguished from deductivism with respect to fundamental moral principles. The latter is a method for establishing fundamental norms, but the concern here is with the application of norms however they are established. Deductivists supposedly take fundamental principles of moral theory and apply them directly to moral problems arising in various activities. Their ideal is to deduce a policy or action recommendation from fundamental principles together with statements of fact.[3]

A number of telling criticisms have or can be given of this deductive model. First, it leads to rigid and fixed distinctions and priorities that fail to aid in concrete decision making.[4] One is here reminded of John Rawls' lexical ordering of the liberty, equality of opportunity, and difference principles. But, of course, Rawls does not quite fit this characterization; his priority obtains only after a certain level of well-being is achieved, and he indicates that even then the lexical ordering is an oversimplification.[5] Second, there is no classification of facts that enables one simply to apply a rule or principle; facts do not come neatly labeled for the application of rules and principles.[6] Third, deductivists are not responsive to the values intrinsic to the contexts in which problems arise. Their accounts of problems often ignore the wider cultural and historical context. By focusing on the values or norms encapsulated in their own moral theories, other basic considerations or values are often ignored.[7] Fourth, deductivists assume that their moral theories are adequate,[8] and consequently will not amend their theories, no matter how bizarre the results. Thus, one deductivist suggests that in deciding whether to have a child, a couple should consider the happiness that might be had by all the other children that might be procreated instead as well as the effects of each such birth upon the happiness of all existing people.[9] Fifth, deductivists assume that justification takes the form of logical deduction, of assuming cases under fixed rules.[10] However, this model of reasoning has been strongly criticized in both philosophy of science and ethics.

What, then, is the alternative model offered by the internal critics? Even if the deductivist model has significant flaws, one might stick with it in the absence of a better alternative. Often, no alternative is offered. However, a few have suggested a pragmatic eclectic alternative basically stemming from John Dewey's moral theory.[11] Dewey's theory, in a nutshell, is that ethical problems arise in concrete situations when conflicting aims, desires, or inclinations prevent action. The point of ethical analysis is to resolve the conflicts in a way that enables action to proceed.[12] According to the pragmatic eclecticists, one should thus examine the various desires, aims, and values that create a concrete problem. One then formulates alternative plans of action or policies and reflects upon the relevant desires, values, and aims in order to revise them in a way to allow an option to be accepted.[13] There is "no absolute or formulated way to decide such issues,"[14] for the various situations differ and one must reconcile the values and desires in the particular context. At best, moral theory provides suggestions to be used in analyzing particular problems by indicating past thinking on concrete problems, the meaning of the principles,[15] and considerations to be taken into account.[16] No one theory is used or followed.[17] "Our view is not a 'system' but an eclectic combination of insights of a common-sense kind gathered from central schools of ethics. . . . It seems to us to be an intuitive view as it stands."[18]

Does this pragmatic eclecticism provide a useful way to proceed in applied ethics? It has a number of serious difficulties. First, its goal is conflict resolution, not determining what is ethically obligatory, permissible, or wrong. No basis is provided for determining what resolution of aims and desires is appropriate, except that the proposed policy be acceptable upon reflection to those involved.[19] Whatever people agree to, without the usual restrictions of rationality and voluntariness, is acceptable. This seems to imply that if people in a situation think that something is morally permissible, then it is. For a resolution allowing action to proceed, it must be acceptable to all those having power to prevent the action. Consequently, the method provides no grounds for arguing that a situation is not someone's business if that person has the power and desire to intervene. For example, if an employer wants to dictate aspects of an employee's private life, there is no basis for claiming that is not the employer's affair.

Second, because the goal is simply conflict resolution rather than an ethically correct one, the values, aims, and desires of various people in a particular context are accepted at face value. Thus, all sorts of irrational or unjustified factors will have to be taken into account, for no principles are provided to determine which are more or less worthy of recognition. Yet, some work in applied ethics has been concerned to show that particular desires causing conflicts and problems are not worthy of consideration. For example, some scholars have challenged the importance of the desire to have genetic offspring, an often strong desire in questions of population policy, sterilization, and artificial insemination.[20] Others have argued against assigning any weight to so-called external preferences—desires for the assignment of benefits and losses to others.[21] Some recent work in ethical theory has attempted to provide a method for determining which desires are rational and worthy of consideration and which are irrational and to be ignored.[22] Perhaps this criticism is too strong; perhaps principles of moral theory are to be used as rough guides as to which desires and aims are to count. Even so, unless these guides are made explicit, one never knows what is or is not relevant. In short, at worst this method takes as relevant whatever desires, aims, and concerns people may have, no matter how irrational or immoral, and at best it evaluates them on unstated, vague, or *ad hoc* grounds.

Third, the method may lack a requirement of consistency. As some advocates of pragmatic eclecticism have written, "While we consider it salutary to seek logical consistency in ethical positions on similar issues . . . we recognize that historical and social considerations make that virtually impossible."[23] Thus, one can use one set of moral principles for one situation and another for a similar one. However, other advocates may require universalizability so that similar situations are treated similarly.

Fourth, the consistency that results from universalizability is not satisfactory because of the inadequate criterion of relevant similarities. Consistency merely requires that relevantly similar situations be treated similarly. The goal of conflict resolution implies that the values, aims, and desires of those people involved that can prevent acceptance of a policy are relevant. Consequently, so long as someone's desires vary from one situation to another, the situations are relevantly different. Obviously, sometimes people's desires do make a difference as to what ought to be done; for example, whether a physician should sterilize a patient depends upon the patient's desires. However, on the pragmatic eclectic approach, situations can also be relevantly different because of the physician's desires. With two similar patients not wanting steriliza-tion but confronting two different physicians, one might be sterilized and another not, simply because one physician strongly desires sterili-zation for population or eugenic reasons and will not accept any resolu-tion that does not involve sterilization. Pragmatic eclectics have no basis for discounting the physician's desire or for providing an ethical resolution the physician will not accept, because they are not concerned with an ethically correct resolution.

Fifth, some pragmatic eclectic critics suggest or imply that funda-mental moral principles do not make a difference. For example, one au-thor suggests that in determining population policy one can bypass the question of an obligation to future generations. He suggests that one might get along with holding that the end of every generation is to its own well-being.[24] The author fails to recognize that if no obligation to future generations exists, then there simply is no need to worry about the consequences of population growth, nuclear waste, or environmen-tal deterioration beyond at most a century from now when the members of the present generation are dead. It is not only important whether an obligation to future generations exists, but also, if it does, precisely what that obligation involves. An obligation merely to allow survival is less difficult to fulfill than an obligation to permit a quality of life as good as or better than the present one. To claim that these arid philoso-phers' questions are irrelevant is mere conceptual blindness.

Moreover, the dispute over them is not irrelevant to present controver-sies. Some people in well-developed countries deny that there is any duty or obligation to aid less developed ones, and others that it is not even desirable to do so. The same applies to support for the elderly in an aging society. A significant segment of the North American public holds that younger people have no duty or obligation to pay taxes to support the elderly, that it is unjust to require them to do so, and that therefore only private, voluntary pension plans are justifiable. Even on their own view, pragmatic eclecticists should take such views into account. They are committed to giving these views some weight rather than evaluating their correctness, for "there is no overriding 'correct' ethical system."[25]

Even ignoring these basic flaws in the method of pragmatic eclecti-cism as described by its proponents, one must consider whether its ac-tual practice is an improvement over work it decries. So far, few results of the pragmatic eclectic method have appeared, but at least one com-parison can be made between that approach and an allegedly deductivist one with respect to guidelines for population policy.[26] Such a comparison shows that the pragmatic eclecticist approach reaches basically the same conclusions as the allegedly deductivist approach did seven years earlier. The chief difference is that the earlier study provides a theoretical argument for believing its principles are ethically correct.

In sum, the suggested pragmatic eclecticism does not offer a viable method. It does not seek ethically correct principles, only those that will in fact be accepted and resolve conflicts. It accepts without criticism the values, aims, and desires of people involved in a problem, that is, those who can prevent or influence action. It may not require consistency, and even if it does, has no adequate criterion of relevant similarity. It is conceptually blind to the import of radically different moral premises. And it has not yet produced any more specific or useful results than other methods.

Lessons from Legal Reasoning

The dispute over the proper method of applied ethics has interesting parallels with disputes about legal reasoning. In the early part of this century, it was academically popular to condemn mechanical jurisprudence, which was alleged to be the deductive application of legal rules and principles to cases. Such legal reasoning, it was alleged, was overly rigid and insensitive to the values in the particular context. These are essentially the charges made against deductivism in applied ethics.

In place of mechanical jurisprudence, at least in the United States, legal realism became the preferred model. As with pragmatic eclecticism, legal realism grew out of the philosophy of John Dewey. The legal realists emphasized sociological, economic, and other empirical aspects of cases. One had to analyze cases in terms of the values involved, especially the values of the parties in dispute, with some eye to social policy. Among the more moderate legal realists, legal rules were consigned to the role of rough and ready guides that could be avoided whenever the contextual values indicated that it was best to do so. Other realists completely abandoned rules and claimed that one should focus upon what courts in fact do.

These strictures closely parallel those urged by pragmatic eclecticists: one must start with the values of the parties in the actual historical, economic, and cultural context; moral principles are at best general guidelines that can and should be used only in a rough and ready way, giving way to competing considerations. Instead of worrying about moral principles, it is best to look at concrete situations so that experienced reality can be the basis for decision.

The history of the arguments over mechanical jurisprudence and legal realism is instructive for models of applied ethics. A careful and detailed examination of the work of the alleged advocates or practitioners of mechanical jurisprudence, such as John Austin, failed to confirm that they held such a theory.[27] A similar result stems from a close examination of the work of alleged deductivists in applied ethics. There are few examples of deductivist reasoning and hardly anyone uses deductivist reasoning most of the time.

Legal realism itself came under increasing attack and has now largely disappeared. Even if legal rules and principles do not mechanically determine conclusions in particular cases, there surely is a difference between a judge trying to apply a rule and one simply making up decisions for particular cases without any such guidance.[28] While legal decisions are not a deductive application of rules to cases, they are also not mere unreasoned responses determined more by the looks of the defendant and the state of the judge's digestive system than by legal considerations. Several features of legal reasoning are now more or less agreed upon by scholars. These features might be useful suggestions for an appropriate method in applied ethics. Both the law and applied ethics are concerned to determine normatively correct conduct in problematic situations. First, facts do not come neatly labeled and categorized, and an important element in legal reasoning is the classification of facts in light of legal principles and rules.[29] Second, even with the facts so categorized, one cannot simply apply a rule; one must often take into account the broader perspective of a statute or policy.[30] Third, courts develop legal principles and doctrines from a series of actual cases. These legal principles do not simply determine a correct solution; they often provide one consideration that must be weighed or balanced against another.[31]

Appellate courts are largely engaged in working out and applying midlevel bridging principles to mediate between abstract theory and actual cases. The United States Constitution's first amendment guarantee of freedom of speech is not simply applied directly to settle a case. Instead, various bridging principles are developed, such as clear and present danger or balancing tests. Which bridging principle one chooses in part depends upon one's theory of the Constitution. Moreover, the configuration of these bridging principles is apt to change as one determines their effects upon various values in concrete cases. That is, principles are modified over time as a result of examining their concrete applications. Thus, from being almost outside the freedom of speech protection, advertising has been seen to be important in informing people of opportunities to exercise other fundamental freedoms, such as the right to abortion or the services of a lawyer.[32]

Of course many differences exist between legal and moral reasoning. Applied ethics is not committed to any doctrine of predecent; it does not have precisely worded statutes to interpret. One important consequence of these differences (among others) is that it is easier for reasonable people to differ in ethics. There are fewer clear-cut rules. Much more moral reasoning is a matter of comparing, balancing, weighing, and reconciling competing considerations. Nonetheless, many clear-cut cases exist, such as the wrongness of reducing population growth by deliberately withholding medicine during epidemics in order to raise the mortality rate, or the wrongness of not informing a patient that he or she has influenza. But these unproblematic cases, like many of those in lower courts, are uninteresting. The emphasis in applied ethics, as in appellate courts, is upon those in which the facts are complicated, the issues are new, or competing considerations make them a close call. Thus, disagreement can be expected in the areas of concern in applied ethics. Nonetheless, as in court cases, argument and reflection tend to focus and narrow the range of dispute. The viable options are reduced and the differences become fewer. Of course, these differences are dramatic in particular cases, a respirator is or is not turned off, just as in court cases the defendant is or is not liable. There simply become fewer types of cases in which disagreement persists.

A THIRD METHOD

An appropriate method of applied ethics must steer a course in the deeper channel between the twin shoals of deductivism and pragmatic eclecticism. Four general features of legal reasoning provide guidance for such a methodology. First, as in appellate courts with discretionary review, cases or topics chosen should be actual disputes of broad importance. Well-settled issues are not usually heard again. Second, factual information must be obtained, classified, and considered in relation to different values, principles, and policies. Third, and most important, midlevel principles must be formulated, balanced against one another, and be open to revision in light of new considerations. Fourth, critical cases are judged by appeals to rules and principles. These four features—choice of topics, marshaling of facts, development of midlevel bridging principles, and evaluation of cases—are central to applied ethics.

Topics

Applied ethics cannot be useful if it fails to address appropriate problems. Three specific mistakes should be avoided in choosing problems. First, moral philosophers sometimes address unreal or nonexistent problems. For example, in a volume on world hunger, one author discusses whether food ought to be shared equally even if everyone in the world would starve.[33] Only in the penultimate paragraph does he admit that such an outcome would never occur. As more and more people starved to death, a point would be reached when enough food would exist for the remaining people to survive.

A second mistake is to focus on rare, dramatic problems. For example, a recent book in bioethics takes as an example whether a physician should accede to a female patient's request to have one of her well-developed breasts reduced in size because it inhibits her golf swing.[34] Although this is an actual case, a family physician remarked that it would not help his students develop methods for their everyday problems. Probably more ink has been spilt in population ethics on the brief period of compulsory sterilization in India than on any other issue. Ethicists should try to anticipate problems and address them before they become widespread, but many of those that have been addressed will permanently affect only a tiny minority of the population.

Third, philosophers have often attacked dead issues. For example, it was not until after the 1973 United States Supreme Court abortion decision that a spate of articles by philosophers appeared addressing whether abortion should be legally permissible. Prior to that decision, they largely ignored the issue. Similarly, articles about the Constitution requiring the government to fund abortions started to appear only after the Supreme Court had decided that issue. Too often, philosophers appear to be offering rationalizations for existing practices.[35] Some people will object that these are not dead issues, that abortion is a very central conflict in society. However, while there are many live abortion issues, such as whether Congress and legislatures should fund abortions, the Constitutional issues are certainly less so. After all, the last Constitutional amendment overturning a Supreme Court decision was in 1913 adopting the income tax, and some people think a Constitutional amendment allowing school prayers is still a live issue. In any case, regardless of the specific example, effort is not well devoted to issues after they have been practically settled.

The problems that should be addressed are the opposite of those involved in these mistakes, that is, real, common, live problems. These are the ones that affect most people. And there are plenty of them available. In the population field, little has been written on whether population aid programs should or should not adapt to the differing cultural values in less developed countries; whether population aid may ethically be tied to other forms of aid, and if so, under what conditions; whether and to what extent population aid donors should respect the sovereignty of recipient countries and even what that means; what constitutes a fair and equitable immigration policy; and what sorts of policies are ethically justifiable with respect to the elderly in aging societies such as the United States and Canada.

There are also many unanalyzed or insufficiently analyzed ethical issues in bioethics and professional ethics. For example, should anesthetists obtain separate informed consent, or is consent to surgery sufficient because everyone knows anesthesia is administered during surgery? What policy should be adopted, if any, with respect to home births or delivery by lay and nurse midwives? And in professional ethics, whistle blowing and providing bribes in foreign countries are not the sole issues. One might also examine strikes by professionals, whether professionals should be required to inform clients when they make mistakes, or what constitutes an acceptable risk and who is to decide.

Marshaling Facts

Having chosen a problem that is worthy of analysis, one must both gather factual information[36] and classify it in terms of its ethical relevance. Gathering information is a rather complicated matter. Few ethicists today use incorrect facts; but it is still easy to take the traditional philosopher's gambit and argue on a supposition that the facts are as one describes. The problem with that approach in applied ethics, as opposed to arguments about the adequacy of a moral theory, is that one may then make a major contribution to the resolution of a nonexistent problem. Moreover, although correct, the information may be seriously incomplete, failing to provide an adequate understanding of the problem.

A minimum requirement to working on a problem in applied ethics is to have read some of the important nonphilosophical literature in the field. An often beneficial secondary technique is to work with, or at least discuss the problem with, people who are not philosophers but actively involved in concrete situations. Some ethics institutes try to involve people from a variety of disciplines in their projects, but that is not possible for all the people who might contribute to applied ethics. If ethicists are at universities, people in other disciplines are usually willing at least to read drafts of papers or discuss problems. The involvement of people from other disciplines, however, cannot replace having some knowledge acquired on one's own.

The most difficult question is how helpful practical experience can be. Some graduate programs in bioethics now emphasize practical clinical experience. The claim is that clinical experience provides access to factual information one cannot obtain in any other way. This claim is ambiguous. On the one hand, it could mean that the information is in principle unobtainable any other way; that it is inexpressible or incommunicable. Even if true, it is unclear how this information will be useful for ethical analysis to be communicated to others. On the other hand, it could mean that as a matter of fact much information is not otherwise available. For example, one might appeal to the limited work available in medical sociology. This claim has some plausibility, but its truth will depend upon the topic and the current state of the literature. Moreover, on this interpretation, practical experience is not logically necessary. At best, at some times it will be necessary for some problems. One need not have witnessed a sterilization or artificial insemination to write about the ethics of these activities. At the very most, practical experience is necessary for but a few issues.

Thus, practical experience might be useful in providing some otherwise unavailable information needed to analyze and evaluate practical problems. It can also have some possible pitfalls. First, for a couple of reasons, brief practical exposure might not be typical. Those practitioners willing to take on students are not likely to be a representative sample. Among physicians, they are apt to be especially aware of ethical questions and thus treat their patients differently from most physicians. They are apt to be much more sensitive than a physician who saw no difficulty about the capacity of subjects to consent to experimental drug therapy, even though many of them did not know the day of the week or what a fork was for. Moreover, limited clinical experience may not provide a typical view of the general pattern of professional practice.

A second possible pitfall of practical experience is that one can become co-opted. One can easily assume and accept the working presuppositions of those with whom one associates. For example, in recommending how clinical experience and factual information can assist in applied ethics, one author gives as an illustration not telling a terminally ill fifteen year old girl of the alternatives to blood transfusion, because of the "possible anxieties" which would be involved in "discussing alternative ways her terminal event might occur." [37] This example illustrates the traditional biases of physicians against informing patients of terminal illnesses. And if one comes to perceive problems and situations as practitioners do, radical critiques of their views and moral assumptions are not likely.

On the other hand, ethical views resting upon mistaken factual assumptions can be corrected by practical experience. For example, one philosopher believed that no one is mentally ill; that mental illness is a myth. After working one summer at an institution for the mentally ill, he came to believe that some people really are mentally ill. But such "revelations" are probably few.

Finally, practical experience can, though it need not, lead to emotional involvement that biases one's perspective, [38] although remaining in the study is no guarantee against bias. Adequate ethical evaluation requires an independent and objective assessment of the realities involved. Of course, this does not mean an uncaring, unconcerned, or unsympathetic point of view. Nor does it mean that emotions have no role in morality. Yet, much contemporary public discussion of moral questions involves a passion and bias that distorts judgment. Anyone who works with a disadvantaged group is likely to develop a sympathy and advocacy on their behalf that does not take cognizance of the similar situation of others. This can lead to ethical claims that cannot be consistently supported. For example, advocates for mentally retarded persons argue for changes in zoning laws to permit multiple family housing in areas zoned for single families. However, once one argues for changes in zoning regulations for mentally retarded persons, one might not be able to provide a principled reason why such changes should not also be made for the elderly, battered wives, the mentally ill, former drug addicts, and ex-convicts. This is not to say consistent positions cannot be defended, only that emotionally involved advocates often do not perceive the need for considering other similar groups and developing a consistent policy based solely upon ethically relevant differences, because all their attention is focused on the immediate problems of those with whom they work.

Once one has empirical knowledge of a type of problem, one must classify facts for ethical evaluation. This involves two processes. First, one examines the empirical situation in order to classify various sorts of possible outcomes in terms of their ethical relevance. For example, is it ethically relevant or important that if women can use prenatal diagnosis and selective abortion to determine the sex of their children this will lead to a sex imbalance in the population? Why would a sex imbalance be good or bad? Here the principles or values of moral theory are relevant. For example, in itself a sex imbalance is not morally important, but it might lead to unhappiness due to the absence of available mates. The classification cannot be completed at this stage, but some preliminary indications are needed.

One can also make a preliminary classification of policies or actions based on how they affect values or principles. Thus, in population policy one can group family planning, withholding or preventing access to services, positive incentives, negative incentives, and compulsion or peer pressure according to different values that might be affected. For example, positive and negative incentives have a similar impact upon equality, but importantly different ones on freedom. At this point, moral theory fills one of the significant gaps in the pragmatic eclectic method; it indicates which moral principles or values are most relevant in considering policies and actions.

At this point, one cannot usually establish priorities among the various values or moral principles. Almost all moral theories require some trade-off or balancing among morally relevant considerations or effects. The abstract rights in a natural rights theory must be more precisely defined and comparatively evaluated in order to be made compatible. A theory of prima facie duties has to decide which of several relevant ones is the most stringent. While utilitarians do not have to trade off different values, they do have to weigh and balance one set of consequences against others. Perhaps only a strict Kantian theory avoids having to reconcile or compare values, principles, or effects. And even contemporary versions of Kant, whether of the form advocated by Rawls or Gewirth, require such trade-offs.[39] Rawls' theory requires considerations of various liberties within the principle of liberty as well as rather detailed considerations as to what will impinge upon the least advantaged; while Gewirth's theory requires some reconciliation of conflicts between rights to freedom and to well-being.

Midlevel Principles

This necessity for some sort of reconciliation of various values, moral principles, or effects leads to the formulation of midlevel bridging principles. This aspect is often overlooked in the deductive method, which tries to go immediately from very general, fundamental moral principles or values to hard and fast rules or decisions. However, an examination of the field of applied ethics shows many important midlevel bridging principles. The principles of informed consent and confidentiality in bioethics are such principles. The bridging principles are often similar from one field to another, because they stem from the same fundamental moral principles applied to different contexts. For example, the principle of the least restrictive alternative for mentally retarded persons is essentially the same as the population policy guideline of preferring policies less restrictive of freedom. Another similar bridging principle is that, except for professional capacities, an agent cannot morally do what a principal cannot morally do. In the population area, this implies that donor agencies cannot morally fund others to carry out programs they are not ethically free to pursue, such as funding abortions. In professional ethics, it means a professional is not morally entitled to perform actions, such as lie, that the client is not morally free to perform. Of course, there are qualifications and exceptions that must be worked out for detailed situations.

The formulation of midlevel bridging principles is the most important, and should be the primary, work of applied ethicists. It is incorrect to think that midlevel principles are all on a par and simply deduced from supreme principles. Midlevel principles can actually involve several levels. For example, the principle that freedom should be respected can be analyzed into a more specific principle concerning freedom of reproduction and that in turn into principles about the freedom to determine the number of children one will have, the freedom to have genetic offspring, the freedom to bear children, and the freedom to rear children. These different subfreedoms are not of the same importance and evaluation must keep them distinct when considering such issues as surrogate motherhood.

Midlevel bridging principles encapsulate important values or considerations of an ethical theory for a broad range of empirical circumstances. For example, a utilitarian can regard a principle of freedom (or a prohibition of coercion) as indicating the tendency of freedom to promote happiness. However, other effects from the exercise of freedom can produce unhappiness. Similarly, informed consent to medical treatment can signify an important consideration promoting happiness on a utilitarian theory or autonomy on a Kantian one. As principles pick out only one general ethical consideration, other principles may pick out considerations leading to opposite conclusions in particular cases. Consequently, midlevel principles provide a bridge between an abstract moral theory and actual cases or problems and must often be weighed against one another.

In formulating midlevel bridging principles, one must often examine in detail a number of specific cases or policies. This does not mean that principles are to be formulated to give results one antecedently determines to be correct by intuition or "gut" feeling. The formulation of midlevel bridging principles is not a simple process of induction, because for induction one must antecedently know what is ethically correct in particular cases, which begs the question.[40] Rather, consideration of particular cases and policies can lead one to see effects on moral values and principles not adequately taken into account in the first formulations of midlevel principles. For example, considerations of privacy and freedom might lead one to formulate principle that information from genetic tests for conditions predisposing to certain diseases should not be released to insurance companies. However, consideration of situations indicates that people predisposed to diseases might take out extra insurance when they learn that they are likely to contract an illness. This would significantly increase the cost of insurance to others, and although insurance is designed to spread costs and risks, this could be unfair. Consequently, the midlevel principle might need to be revised to prevent people taking unfair advantage of medical information about their health status.

The process in developing such midlevel principles is not simple deduction. The values or principles of freedom, privacy, and fairness are all involved. Moreover, privacy and freedom have to be reconciled with preventing unfairness. No straightforward deduction from a supreme moral principle will do this. Instead, the process is one of trying to formulate general statements of significant effects on values.

The weightings assigned to various considerations depend in part upon the particular moral theory used. At the level of bridging principles, different moral theories can support the same principles, but assign them different weights or levels of importance. For example, although both a utilitarian and a Kantian can support confidentiality or truth-telling in the professional-client relationship, a utilitarian might assign these less weight vis-à-vis a client's or another's well-being than would a Kantian concerned with autonomy.

This does not imply, as some critics of applied ethics seem to think, that moral theory cannot be used until an adequate moral theory is developed. One might as well argue that one cannot do engineering until a complete scientific theory is developed. As both a utilitarian and a Kantian will agree on a midlevel principle of confidentiality, disagreement is then confined to those cases in which their different weightings make a difference. Strong disagreement at the theoretical level is reduced at the level of midlevel principles to the borderline and hard cases. Many instances of lying or violation of confidentiality are ruled out as unethical. Progress is made and the areas of disagreement narrowed. Moreover, when one looks at the bulk of situations that actually arise, disagreement affects a very small proportion. Still, without at least some background theory, no general justification of midlevel principles can occur. Only a theory can provide guidance as to what values and effects to use in formulating principles. However, sometimes one need not explicitly refer to the general moral theory; one can proceed, as in the example of information from genetic testing, by appeal to more general midlevel principles.

Cases and Rules

The evaluation of policies or actions is then done as much as possible by midlevel bridging principles. Sometimes one can formulate rules which help reconcile different implications of bridging principles. For example, a professional should never serve two clients whose interests are in direct conflict in a transaction. This rule prohibits a physician attending both the donor and recipient in a transplant operation as well as a lawyer representing both sides in a court case. However, rules of this sort are often not possible because the values in bridging principles can be variously affected. For example, if confidentiality of the professional-client relationship conflicts with avoidance of harm to others, the amounts of loss of confidentiality and of harm to others can vary over a broad spectrum. One cannot plausibly claim that one consideration always overrides the other. Problems of this sort have been the bane of all moral theories that have tried to have absolute prohibitions or duties; cases are not only imaginable but actually occur in which the loss to other principles or values is so great as to outweigh that of the allegedly absolute principle. One can achieve the appearance of absolutism by building in exceptions or more narrowly circumscribing principles, but this is the result of the comparison, balancing, weighing, or reconciling of conflicting considerations. The absolute principle did not come so neatly defined and bounded. Thus, if one is working out a view rather than merely following one already completely determined, one cannot avoid the process of comparing, weighing, balancing, or reconciling. Deductivism confuses the conclusions with the process of formulating conclusions and thus fails to modify principles in light of their implications for particular situations.

EXPECTATIONS AND EFFECTIVENESS

Given this methodology of applied ethics, what can one legitimately expect from it? First, one can expect some clarification of what is relevant to problems. This should result from using moral theory to sort out the various morally relevant empirical facts. Sometimes this is all that is needed. For example, some psychiatrists and others involved in mental institutions have been concerned about the effects of deinstitutionalization. Former patients often live in poor and squalid conditions. Thus, some mental health workers have wondered whether former patients might not be better off being recommitted to institutions. One must sort out the reasons for recommitments. These can be the mental condition of the patients or their poverty—bad housing and poor diet. If the latter is the reason for recommitting people, then it would be a reason for institutionalizing all poor people. If the reason is not simply that they are poor but that they are also former mental patients, then one seems to be discriminating against them because they are former mental patients. Thus, it quickly becomes clear that the only acceptable ethical reason for recommitting former patients is their mental health. This provides a relatively useful guide for determining how many former inpatients are actually suffering important decreases of mental health as a result of being released. Even granting the variability of psychiatric evaluations, this class will certainly be smaller than and different from the class of former patients who are badly housed and fed.

Second, one can expect the development of some midlevel bridging principles. The previous example of deinstitutionalization of mental patients came close to formulating a bridging principle. Various other examples have been given throughout this essay, so there is little need to expand on them. However, these bridging principles must not be thought unimportant. They provide the operating principles for much moral evaluation of policies and actions. Nevertheless, one cannot operate with them alone. Reference to moral theory is still needed to indicate their bases—why they are important—so that they can be balanced against one another, and to fill in gaps where bridging principles are unavailable or are inadequate because they do not cover all relevant considerations.

Third, sometimes one can expect to arrive at rules that do not provide considerations to be balanced against one another but specific directives for a class of cases.[41] Rules often reflect a stable balancing of different principles; they can be formulated only for types of situations where the weights of various considerations do not vary greatly. For example, one can make a rule that a physician should never refuse to treat one of his or her patients, but one cannot justify a rule specifying precisely how many patients a physician should accept.

Fourth, one can sometimes expect procedures to help decide on particular actions or policies. Procedures can be of two types—conceptual or institutional. Conceptual procedures provide ways of framing and thinking through decisions. For example, if one must choose between two courses of action that provide benefits and losses to different people, one can sometimes decide on the basis of which set of benefits and losses one would choose were they both to accrue to oneself.[42] Institutional procedures are often simply ways to get an acceptable comparison or weighing of competing considerations. Examples of such procedures abound. Institutional review boards for human experimentation are one such example, for they are to weigh the risks and benefits of experiments. Local advisory groups for population programs are another, though they also fulfill the important function of providing input for relevant empirical information. Safety review committees for engineering design are another institutional mechanism for determining whether the risks involved are acceptable. Not all institutional procedures need involve committees. They can merely involve having items checked by another person or even a simple checklist to make certain one has considered all factors.

Fifth, one can expect a narrowing of the range of disagreement. Although disagreement will often persist over particular cases, it is likely to be less than that at the level of moral theory. Utilitarians and Kantians are in radical disagreement at the theoretical level, Kantians holding that right and wrong is independent of consequences and utilitarians holding that only consequences count. Yet, as previously indicated, they can agree on principles of informed consent, confidentiality, and truthfulness. Their disagreement at this level is a matter of relative weighting of these principles. At the level of particular cases, they will agree over a wide range, probably most actual behavior. Disagreement is then limited to borderline cases. In a number of group studies by people of quite different moral perspectives, agreement has been reached.[43]

If these are the main results one can expect from applied ethics, then how effective can it be? To answer such a question, one must be more precise about effectiveness. One must first answer the question: Effective at what? One answer would be effective at providing just the results that can reasonably be expected. Applied ethics can be rather effective in this respect. The literature is full of proposed institutional and conceptual mechanisms, midlevel bridging principles, recommended weightings, clarifications of relevant considerations, and so forth. However, it is doubtful that this is what people who ask about the effectiveness of applied ethics have in mind.

Sometimes people mean by effective the providing of specific decisions, such as whether aggressive treatment should be provided this patient, or whether Singapore's policy of mixed positive and negative incentives for reducing fertility is justified. This question of effectiveness is never asked of easy cases. If the patient is irreversibly comatose, the answer to aggressive therapy is fairly clear. People only ask about the effectiveness of applied ethics where the competing considerations or complex of facts make the decision unclear or a close call. Applied ethics cannot provide a clear-cut decision procedure that easily grinds out answers for all situations, no matter how hard or borderline they may be. To ask for that is to ask for a mechanical deductivism. Such methods are found only in mathematics and a few other fields. Economics and medicine do not give clear-cut decision procedures for all financial investments or treatments for illnesses, only for the easy ones. There will always be borderline and hard cases either because the situations are complex, the issues are new, or the competing considerations are very closely in balance. The exercise of moral judgment will always be necessary.

However, applied ethics can make some hard cases easier. The use of midlevel principles can often rule out options that were previously thought open. Moreover, conceptual clarification can sometimes make an issue clear. Applied ethics can also help clarify how strong an argument is for a particular choice. Nonetheless, ethicists are not trained for on the spot judgments. It is ludicrous for a hospital to have an ethicist on a beeper for call to the bedside to make instant thumbs up or thumbs down decisions. The work of ethics involves careful and detailed analysis and reflection, precisely what is not possible in the practical world.

Hence, while ethicists can sometimes handle hard cases better than practitioners, their relative strength is not at the level of action. Rather, the role of applied ethics is to reflect upon such situations and help practitioners be clearer about what to look for and how much weight to assign to considerations when they must make decisions. Ethicists are not specialists on a par with perinatologists, tax lawyers, and structural engineers.

One can also ask whether applied ethics can be or has been effective in influencing conduct and policy choices. This is the question people usually have in mind when they ask whether applied ethics is effective. Unfortunately, the answer to it is less clear than to the other two questions about effectiveness. In answering it, one must first distinguish, roughly and only roughly, three levels at which applied ethics might be influential. One level is that of governmental policy, from general policies toward development and pensions for the elderly to specific policies like funding abortions through medicaid and zoning to allow multi-family dwellings for persons living with a mental handicap. Another level is that of the practice or policies of organizations such as hospitals, associations of professionals, and organizations on behalf of various disadvantaged groups such as those for retarded or elderly citizens. The last level is that of individual decision making. Here one is concerned with a physician or nurse giving information to a patient, a lawyer refusing to act on behalf of an immoral client, or an official designing a population program.

In general, applied ethics is more effective the lower the level of generality. Thus, it is easier to influence the conduct of an individual than an organization, and an organization than governmental policy or laws. This observation is generally true of anyone attempting to influence conduct, whether on economic, medical, legal, or any other grounds. Nonetheless, applied ethics appears to have had some influence at all three levels. At the governmental policy level, the contribution of applied ethics to the United States National Commission for the Protection of Human Subjects of Biomedical and Behavioral Research was significant, and the Commission's studies have resulted in a few changes in government guidelines. Similarly, articles on applied ethics are occasionally used and cited by government groups recommending changes in laws. Some hospitals and other organizations have altered their practices or policies as a result of work in applied ethics. And, of course, many physicians and other professionals have altered their conduct to be less paternalistic as a result of discussions in applied ethics. One notable example is that none of the major centers for genetic screening in Canada now requires a woman to agree to abortion should Down's syndrome be determined by prenatal diagnosis, although some hospitals may still do so.[44] The work of The Hastings Center in New York has been quite influential in all these respects.[45] Yet, in many situations, one cannot point to any one article or work in applied ethics that has made the difference. Often it has been the result of a growing consensus on midlevel bridging principles that narrows the range of disagreement.

Nevertheless, it is fair to say that the influence of applied ethics has not been all for which one might have hoped. In part, this is because of mistakes in choices of problems, for example, working on dead or exotic issues. In part, it is due to a poor methodology so that the work is not useful, in particular, a failure to develop midlevel bridging principles. And in part it is due to a failure to write in a language understandable to persons in diverse fields without formal training in ethics. The influence of applied ethics depends upon the power and soundness of the reasoning involved, because ethicists are not, fortunately, philosopher kings. If ethical reasoning is to influence others, it must be communicated to them in a form they can understand. If applied ethics is to be influential, it must address real practical problems, develop midlevel bridging principles, and communicate them and the reasons on which they rest to a nonphilosophical public. This can be done, but it has not been done as well as it can be.[46]

NOTES

1. Drucker, "Ethical Chic."

2. The term "application," it may be objected, biases the whole discussion, for it suggests that moral theory is developed and then routinely applied to various cases, which the internal critics deny is the appropriate method. However, it is used instead of "practice" because the latter term suggests a broader scope than is here intended. The concern is what type of advice or recommendations ethicists can provide people in practice, not how people translate it into action. Moreover, it is not assumed that ethicists are necessarily philosophers; some very good ones are lawyers, theologians, or physicians, among others. It is assumed that applied ethics is reflective analysis and writing.

3. Ackerman, "What Bioethics Should Be," p. 269. See also Arthur Caplan, "Applying Morality to Advances in Biomedicine: Can and Should This Be Done?" in *New Knowledge*, ed. Bondeson et al, p. 157; and Noble, "Ethics and Experts," p. 9.

4. Berelson and Lieberson, "Government Efforts to Influence Fertility," pp. 599–601.

5. Rawls, *Theory of Justice*, pp. 44, 45, 542.

6. Hart, "Positivism and the Separation of Law and Morals," p. 607; Hart, *Concept of Law*, p. 123.

7. Ackerman, "What Bioethics Should Be," p. 271; Berelson and Lieberson, "Government Efforts to Influence Fertility," p. 603; Noble, "Ethics and Experts," p. 8; Lieberson, "Book Review," p. 128.

8. Caplan, "Applying Morality," in *New Knowledge*, ed. Bondeson et al., p. 160; Caplan, "Ethical Engineers Need Not Apply," p. 27.

9. Hare, "Abortion and the Golden Rule," p. 218.

10. Caplan, "Ethical Engineers Need Not Apply," p. 30; Caplan, "Applying Morality," in *New Knowledge*, ed. Bondeson et al., pp. 159–60; Noble, "Ethics and Experts," p. 9.

11. Ackerman, "What Bioethics Should Be," p. 260 n.; Berelson and Lieberson, "Government Efforts to Influence Fertility," p. 597 n. 41.

12. Dewey, *Human Nature and Conduct*. Pragmatic eclecticism is not a doctrine Dewey would have accepted.

13. Ackerman, "What Bioethics Should Be," pp. 263–66.

14. Berelson and Lieberson, "Government Efforts to Influence Fertility," p. 604. See also Ackerman, "What Bioethics Should Be," p. 268.

15. Ackerman, "What Bioethics Should Be," p. 270.

16. Lieberson, "Book Review," p. 128.

17. Berelson and Lieberson, "Government Efforts to Influence Fertility," p. 605.

18. Ibid., p. 596.

19. Ackerman, "What Bioethics Should Be," pp. 264–65.

20. Joseph Ellin, "Sterilization, Privacy, and the Value of Reproduction," in *Contemporary Issues*, ed. Davis, Hoffmaster and Shorten, pp. 109–25.

21. Dworkin, *Taking Rights Seriously*, pp. 234–35.

22. Brandt, *Theory of the Good and the Right*. 23. Berelson and Lieberson, "Government Efforts to Influence Fertility," p. 603.

24. Lieberson, "Book Review," p. 126.

25. Berelson and Lieberson, "Government Efforts to Influence Fertility," p. 596.

26. Ibid., p. 596; Daniel Callahan, "Ethics and Population Limitation," in *Ethics and Population*, ed. Bayles, pp. 19–40.

27. Hart, "Positivism and the Separation of Law and Morals," pp. 607–11.

28. Hart, *Concept of Law*, pp. 140–41.

29. Hart, "Positivism and the Separation of Law and Morals," p. 607.

30. Fuller, "Positivism and Fidelity to Law," pp. 664–67.

31. Dworkin, *Taking Rights Seriously*, pp. 22–28.

32. See *Bigelow v. Virginia* and *Bates v. State Bar of Arizona*.

33. Richard A. Watson, "Reason and Morality in a World of Limited Food," in *World Hunger*, ed. Aiken and LaFollette, pp. 115–23.

34. Pence, *Ethical Options in Medicine*, pp. 190–91.

35. See Noble, "Response."

36. Caplan, "Ethical Engineers Need Not Apply," pp. 28–29; Noble, "Ethics and Experts," p. 8.

37. Ackerman, "What Bioethics Should Be," p. 274 n. 9.

38. See Wikler, "Ethicists, Critics, and Expertise," p. 12.

39. Rawls, *Theory of Justice*; Gewirth, *Reason and Morality*.

40. See Kant, *Moral Law,*, pp. 74–75, Akademie pagination, pp. 406–7.

41. Dworkin, *Taking Rights Seriously*, pp. 22–28.

42. Bayles, *Morality and Population Policy*, p. 64; Bayles, *Professional Ethics*, pp. 100–101.

43. See, for example, Powledge and Fletcher, "Guidelines for the Ethical, Social and Legal Issues in Prenatal Diagnosis."

44. Rubin, "Malpractice Board Urged by MD/Lawyer," p. 17.

45. "The Hastings Center: Ethics in the 80s."

46. Earlier versions of this essay were presented as papers at the Kennedy Institute of Ethics of Georgetown University and the University of Miami. It has also benefited from comments by Bruce Chapman, Benjamin Freedman, and Barry Hoffmaster.

2

Ethics Applied Or *Conduct Enlightened?*
Abraham Edel

I recall my philosophical excitement in coming on Wayne Leys' book, *Ethics for Policy Decisions*, in the early 1950s. Of course, the idea that ethical theory should be applied to moral tasks is a venerable one. But, the notion that to labor in the vineyards of the moral guidance of conduct requires recasting ethical theory itself and reinterpreting its functions and processes was a rude shock to moral philosophers claiming their domain was an isolated metaethics. Metaethics, you will recall, was conceived as purely linguistic-logical analysis of moral discourse, a self-enclosed field quite apart from the "preaching" and "exhortation" of substantive or normative ethics, and in no way beholden to these practical tasks for methods or conclusions.

This Age of Analysis that had come to dominate the Anglo-American philosophical scene sometime in the 1930s came to an end in the 1970s, at least for moral philosophy. Today moral philosophers consider bioethics, technological and environmental ethics, ethics and social policy, and are tilling with fresh energy the older fields of business and legal ethics. With the economic pressure of current retrenchment in the academy, they have undertaken philosophical internships in hospitals and small communities and even in the halls of Congress. Institutes and centers and journals of applied ethics or ethics and public policy are springing up at many points in the United States and Canada (e.g., Maryland, Delaware, Colorado, Texas, Florida, and London, Ontario) as well as abroad. The whole field is commonly referred to as "Applied Ethics."

Consider this notion of Applied Ethics as a problem in the relation of theory and practice. Such a burgeoning field makes it important to see clearly what is happening in what is thought of as application. The point is not simply to clarify the meaning of the term "applied" but to make sure that old ideas, attitudes, and models that may lurk in so broad a concept do not by some silent entrenchment rob us of the fruits of the new expansion of moral philosophy.

Since the notion of application is so broad or loose, one has to ask what is being applied to what. Three possibly different answers are found in current practice. First, *ethical theory* is being applied to problems of *practice*. Indeed, text-books are appearing in which different ethical approaches are outlined—Kantian, Utilitarian, Natural Rights, and so forth—and then the theories are tried out on typical problems such as abortion, civil disobedience, sexual cohabitation outside of marriage, whistle-blowing, and so on.

A second answer is that ordinary morality, that is, a *common moral code*, is being applied to *some special area or province or profession*. A great deal of what is currently called Applied Ethics is of this sort. A common morality of honesty and respect for persons and property and the rest is taken for granted—as for example the Decalogue within the Hebraic-Christian tradition—and the question is how does that apply to business and technology, medicine and law, education and politics. One might compare this to an ethical empire in which the common morality holds rule and the provinces try to apply its edicts to their special aims.

A third answer is like the second in applying a *common moral code*, but like the first in applying it directly to *particular problems of practice*. It is applying some element in the substantive morality—moral rules or moral principles, ideals or character-models—and it bypasses all provincial divisions to go straight to the moral problems. It is worth noting that some of the Centers today do not make use of the concept of Applied Ethics itself; they use some appellation like "Philosophy and Public Policy" or "Ethics and Social Policy" and, thereby, are able to range over both institutional and special problems and reach more freely beyond the confines of traditional moral philosophy in analyzing particular issues.

Each of these views about what is being applied to what will be considered. Thereafter, since it is possible that resort to the general idea of Applied Ethics is simply following current usage of Applied Science as a model, some aspects of that latter usage will be explored briefly.

MORALITY APPLIED TO INDIVIDUAL PRACTICE

How is an ethical theory applied? As complex affairs, ethical theories contain all sorts of issues of definition, interpretation, and operational procedures in their use. Compare, for example, Utilitarianism and Kantianism. Utilitarianism defines "ought" in terms of "good" so that to say "I ought to do this" is equivalent to "My doing it in the present situation will promote more good than any alternative available act." The Kantians distinguish "good" in a moral sense so that "This action is good" is analyzed as "This is the sort of action a morally good person would do in this situation" and "A morally good person is one who does what he ought to do." The Utilitarians will interpret "good" as pleasure or happiness, and their operational procedure is a felicific calculus, that is, instructions as to how to measure the greatest happiness for the parties concerned. The Kantians, on the other hand, interpret obligation and moral goodness in terms of the exercise of a rational will, and the operational procedure is the familiar self-questioning as to whether one is ready to universalize the maxim on which one is proposing action. This is stated in a way to bring out a contrast of the approaches, but a probing philosophical inquiry is required to check whether there is really an opposition, or whether the theories are just looking in different directions so that uncovering their full content might show they have a great deal in common.[1] Fortunately, that is not the present task. Our present concern is what goes on in application. Let us, therefore, take an example.

Consider the current controversy over safety in one's workplace. On the one hand, growing awareness of the dangers of radiation and other forms of pollution (e.g., chemical) coupled with statistical studies of comparative incidence of cancer and other illnesses now enable us to devise techniques and conditions that would provide greater safety in the workplace. On the other hand, they might often seriously raise the cost of production. Should economic considerations be allowed to enter into the calculations of a regulatory commission that can make safeguards mandatory? The labor unions tend to say no and attack the effort to carry through a "cost-benefit" analysis in such matters; the employers say yes, and argue that we need a full picture of the consequences in order to judge the greatest public well-being.

Now should we say that the unions are applying a Kantian theory of ethics while the employers are applying a Utilitarian theory? After all, Kant speaks of the infinite worth of the human being compared to the finite worth of the ends of desire; it is the Utilitarians who, though they have every person count equally as one, would settle policy in terms of the greatest total happiness of the greatest number of those concerned. Are large groups of consumers among the parties concerned because they could not afford the product if it were not paid for in part by the greater incidence of cancer among the workers, or are they outsiders who are not aware that they are chiseling part of their consumer goods from the health of the workers?

A persistent utilitarian cost-benefit analysis certainly reveals the full scope of the alternatives, and, perhaps, being pressed further, it may provide a moral analysis of the controversy. For example, it might trace what happens to a civilization that is ready to sacrifice a proportion of lives for the benefit of a portion of its people—whether in the workplace, on the highways, in wars and power struggles, and so on. Doubtless this would lead back to the fundamental idea of happiness and what its constituents are, and whether the ethical theory can really use as its operation for a person's good what he or she desires as a subjective matter or votes for.

Utilitarianism would seem to take the long way round—Kant spoke of the "serpentine windings of Utilitarianism"—while the Kantians call for a more direct route. A Kantian might ask why when a child falls down a deep well or a boat is lost at sea we so readily employ all resources for the rescue, even where it means risking others' lives; or why people are so hesitant, in the hospital use of life-extending techniques, to turn them off. Does this not show our moral recognition of the ultimately intrinsic value of the living being? It is the Kantian influence in contemporary philosophy that leads to a view (such as Ronald Dworkin's) that an individual human right can trump the general welfare; or that (as in Rawls' theory of justice) benefit to the most disadvantaged has to be added to the well-being of the majority. But, in construing such qualifications as rejecting Utilitarianism, remember that in earlier moral theory the Utilitarians were the champions of a democratic outlook, for their now limited appeal to the well-being of the greatest number was directed against the monopoly of goods by an established few.

Such consideration of the two ethical theories suggests that we are not really engaged in applying them so much as letting our moral intuitions or reactions clarify and extend or even decide between the theories themselves. And yet, to analyze a situation so that a moral reaction becomes directed requires some theoretical concepts and some operational procedures, in this we are using the instruments that the different theories have to offer. It would seem, then, less a matter of applying theories than of utilizing them as instruments where they help out.

At this point, Wayne Leys' procedure in his book, *Ethics for Policy Decisions*, can come to our assistance. He sketches different ethical theories—Utilitarian, Kantian, Stoic, Pragmatic, Marxian, et al—and, then, offers practical situations and problems on which the theory might shed light. He asks persistently what the theory has brought to the situation, and what deliberative questions it raises. It is a first step. It is not assumed that all theories have always to be raised, nor that there is some single theory that will synthesize them all. As the subtitle of the book —*The Art of Asking Deliberative Questions*—suggests, the initial focus is on the situation that demands policy decision; to ask the proper questions and open up the proper avenues of exploration is an art, and ethical theories are aids in the exercise of that art. That is all that is being done in applying ethical theory.

Note some of the implications of this position. For one thing, the ethical theory surrenders its universal pretensions. The usual theory is assumed to have universal scope. You cannot be a Utilitarian during the week and a Kantian on weekends, or a Stoic on the job and an Epicurean after hours. But why not? Perhaps, on the one hand, some jobs or some areas require a particular mode of analysis and others differ in their requirements. On the other hand, most jobs are complex, and it is more likely that the different modes of analysis will fit different aspects.

There are other possibilities. For example, Nietzsche said that he studied an ethical theory to grasp the kind of personality that found expression in it; he loathed the calculative shopkeeper core of the Benthamite and longed for the heroic. Eduard Spranger in his *Types of Men* correlates ethical systems with a variety of one-sided attitudes: the utility of the economic man, the ethics of legality, the emphasis on inner form of the aesthetic type, the ethics of sociality and loyalty, that of self-affirmation, that of religiosity. And yet in freeing himself from the imposition of any one ethical system, he finds a need to offer a principle of choice and identifies moral autonomy with the demand "Be whatever you can, but be it wholly."

The pressure of theoretical pluralism drives in two directions. One is toward a supertheory which will integrate the partial ones, which will tell us when to use utilitarian techniques, when Kantian firmness, when Stoic resignation, etc. The other is a Deweyan acceptance of the flux of problems and situations in which different theories serve rather as representations of abstract phases and so provide models or instruments to be employed on a criterion of their helpfulness in analyzing and solving the problem.

In either direction, it does not appear fruitful to start with an avowal of a theory and then head for application. No one says "I am a Utilitarian" and therefore cost-benefit analysis is the right and proper thing to do, nor "I am a Kantian" and therefore safety techniques should be introduced into the place of work. Such stances restrict the discussion so that each would try to find grounds in the other's system for pressing its own case. Can you conceive of the workers saying to the employers "But you've forgotten that if you don't put in the devices you may be sued by individuals who have developed cancer, and this may cost you a lot more in the eventual outcome." [2] (This is seen more directly in explosions within mines where safety devices have not been installed, or even more startlingly in the financial consequences of a nuclear episode like that at Three-Mile Island.) Or consider the employer who accepts the Kantian universalization test and shows he is consistent in his claim that the greater risk should be tolerated by moving his own office for daily work onto the factory floor; he is, thus, exposed to the risks as much as his workmen—like a military officer leading the attack rather than ordering it from safe quarters. [3] Neither of these moves really sounds like an ethical resolution: the one is like determining ethical policy in medical ethics through fear of malpractice suits, while the other substitutes an individual for a social solution—it is little consolation when both the employer and the employee suffer the ills that could have been avoided.

On Leys' approach, since what theories have been doing is uncovering selected aspects of the total situation for separate analysis, it is natural to extend the search and seek light from any other available theories. Thus, a Stoic ethics, with its emphasis on resignation, might alert us to the element of unavoidable risk in any complex industrial society. The Stoic Epictetus, seeing no external way of coping with risk, recommends a policy of withdrawing our emotional attachments: do not get so attached to a beautiful ceramic bowl, for it is so readily broken. But life is equally fragile, so he would not have us invest too great a devotion on wife or child or one's own life.

Modern people, with the instrument of statistical theory at hand, are more prone to calculate risks, and so we constantly bet on air and train and motor travel and on working in different industries. Nothing in the Stoic ethics forbids greater control where control is possible—improved control towers and techniques, seatbelts, etc. But the very growth of knowledge that advances control at the same time pinpoints fresh areas of risk: a clear example is genetic knowledge that shows how great an obstacle course has been run by the healthy newborn babe.

Modern people usually depart from the Stoic not in the ideal of how disaster should be faced when it happens but in refusing to make the possibility of disaster the guiding basis of general attitude in life. The Marxian ethical theory draws attention to a quite different aspect of the controversy over safety in the workplace. Focusing on class conflict and the capitalist drive for profit whatever the consequences to the worker, it analyzes the initial appeal to allow the regulatory commission to use cost-benefit analysis as a drive to keep down the costs of production and shift them to the workers. This is on a par with the insistence by the nuclear industry that the government limit the liability of a utility company for nuclear accidents. Hence it should be opposed by labor.

A pragmatic ethics, such as that of Dewey, shares with the utilitarian the desire to become aware of the widest range of consequences. Its normative approach employs intelligence for securing greater human control in solving human problems. Hence, life and health being obvious human ends, social reconstruction is the desirable path where necessary to make available the best knowledge and technique for advancing these ends. Not to make the workplace safer when we know how to do it is like not manufacturing medicines that will cure widespread ills. If vested profits prevent the desired steps, and if the industry is endangered by the added costs, and if the industry is a necessary one and not a luxury, then it may need public help or require public management (as subway or other transportation systems in urban centers often do). Of course such answers may generate other problems that would then have to be faced on their own terms. But to impose the greater risks on the workers—either by threatening to abandon the industry or regarding as inevitable the flight of capital investment to more profitable areas—is morally no different from continuing the deposit of chemical waste in Love Canal to ensure a profitable chemical industry. [4]

The social lesson that part of the costs of production (the so-called "external costs") have been borne unaware by part of the public is a hard-won lesson of social experience. Our century decided earlier that accidents in the workplace were part of the cost of production and systems of workmen's compensation came into being. The same understanding in facing the problem of workmen whom a lifetime of labor left without adequate support for old age led to a system of social security borne in part by the industry that consumed their energies. And we are coming increasingly to see the social capital—accumulated knowledge and technique handed on from the past together with institutions of education and research in the present—as an actual partner in production.

It makes both social and philosophical sense, then, that, in the matter of safety where people work, reconstruction (whether small scale or large scale) is required to ensure safety commensurate with contemporary knowledge of the situation.

Clearly what is going on in all these reflections is not the sheer application of a favored theory to a situation. Rather, a theory is used to clarify, diagnose, structure the situation, not to solve the problem but to prepare the problem for creative solution. Of course, the solution eventually proposed will be guided by an ethical theory, but such theory itself can undergo progressive transformation in experience and in the clarification of values. Hence what at first seemed application of the theory and then seemed simply intuitive moral reaction to its consequences is really a complex interactive experimental process in which moral responses become attuned to refined features and ethical theories become correspondingly revised and elaborated. It is the familiar nonvicious circle of the growth of knowledge.

The history of Utilitarianism is itself a good illustration. As suggested earlier, the slogan of the greatest happiness for the greatest number played a vital role in the ascent of a democratic outlook because it was directed against the dominance of the few. But it became too limited once democracy was established. The history of our last half century is that of liberation movements of minorities (though, in the case of women, actually majorities). If the needs of minorities are to be met, "the greatest number" has to be replaced by a more universal equalitarianism. Theories of human rights of the individual or theories that integrate a reference to gains by the most disadvantaged in any justification of a proposed inequality (as Rawls does) are to be understood as present intellectual experiments that have been only partially successful, for each, as contemporary criticism shows, generates problems of its own. This remains a frontier in ethical theory today, for which the lessons of moral experience in social problems provide strong constraints.

Consider another brief example of how far moral experience penetrates the most arcane parts of an ethical theory. Take the emotive theory of ethics that became popular in the 1930s. Stevenson suggested as models for "This is wrong" and "This is good" respectively *I disapprove of this; do so as well* and *I approve of this; do so as well.*[5] The meaning of ethical terms was, thus, oriented to the affective differences among people and to the struggles that accompanied the phenomenon of ultimate disagreement—a focal issue in the world situation just before World War II.

The emotive theory was criticized by those who had their eye on the consolidation and expansion of what agreement was possible and who utilized the concept of rationality to delineate this aspect. But even within the affective, as war brought other phases of feeling and experience, rival conceptions to emotivism came to the forefront. For example, Sartre suggested that the experience of the resistance movement during the war made "Rather death than . . ." an ultimate experience of the moral.[6] Certainly this was a richer meaning for right and wrong than the emotion of approval plus the effort to impose our feelings on others.

But social experience since the 1940s, particularly of terrorism, has shown the almost promiscuous character of the readiness to sacrifice one's life for a cause. So once again ethical theories that try to integrate the rational and the affective come on the scene. In all these respects ethical theory is itself an advancing frontier, responsive to lessons of changing experience. As it becomes self-conscious it is better able to guide moral efforts to solve our problems.

MORALITY APPLIED TO PARTICULAR SOCIAL PROVINCES

Turn now to the second type of Applied Ethics, in which a common morality is applied to particular social provinces. The use of such terms as "business ethics," "medical ethics," "legal ethics," and so forth is likely to mislead. One may think that one has here different kinds of ethics, rather than a common ethics in different contexts. And yet the different provinces have at times a certain tendency to declare their independence, as if they could pass their own moral laws for their own subjects. Peter Drucker has suggested that fields claim their own ethics when they want to establish rules that are opposed to the common morality. He quotes Bismarck: "What a scoundrel a minister would be if, in his own private life, he did half the things he has a duty to do to be true to his oath of office."[7] And, of course, Machiavellianism is the extreme case of a "political ethics" that goes counter to the precepts of the common morality. So too a "business ethics" can accept bribing a public official in a foreign country so that an American corporation would secure a lucrative contract, even though the same act in the United States would be criminal. This is no novel situation.

Lincoln Steffens, toward the end of his long career, which may be characterized as a search for the ethical, tells in his *Autobiography* of a conversation he had with the president of Harvard. Steffens said he would like to give a course in Law School about the temptations a lawyer meets in his practice. The president assumed this would be directed to teaching them how to avoid sinning. Steffens, I recall, replied something like: no, they have to do these things to succeed and I don't want to stop them from succeeding; I want to show them why it is necessary so they won't feel guilty about doing them. What he really had in mind was to show how the structure of the profession and the conditions of its practice produced the dilemmas. Hence, it was a critique of the institution, not an enshrinement of "sin" as a legal ethics. It is not necessary to add that he was not invited to give the course.

What is one to make of the fact that the common morality says it is wrong to lie and prescribes honesty, while province after province has thought it necessary to water down the prescription? Thus, political ethics takes lightly "mere" campaign promises. Business ethics appears to accept advertising as good-natured exaggeration occasionally stepping over into falsification (it is government that has to impose truth-in-advertising regulation). Journalism and television news readily sacrifice accuracy for the startling scoop. Medicine has often sanctioned keeping the patient in ignorance of the seriousness of his or her condition. Law has many points at which its practitioners may permissibly turn away from a possible truth that is branded irrelevant, and lately enforcing agencies have set dramatic traps for suspected criminals with fabricated, often bizarre, situations. Even religion, in its traditional problems of confidentiality arising out of the confessional, sharpens the concept of a permissible "equivocation." While science itself, which is presumably devoted to truth, on occasion, for example, in psychological experiments dealing with human subjects, has practiced deceit about the object of the experiment, just as anthropologists have used cameras that appear to be directed at some people while really photographing others.[8]

On the face of it, each province may, as Drucker suggests, seem to be setting up its own ethics contrary to the common morality. But in fact it is grappling with a conflict between objectives within its field under the conditions in which they are pursued. This, however, also occurs within common morality itself; for example, the injunction to tell the truth may be morally modulated to spare another's feelings. This is a moral conflict of honesty and compassion; it is not to be compared with an immoral conflict between honesty and private gain. Thus institutionalizing a human activity into a profession or province is not the crucial point. The crucial point lies in conflict of values or responsibilities.

Doubtless a province is generated when in some dependable division of labor some types of enterprise are institutionalized and devoted to more or less well-defined objectives. But the borderline between such provinces and the relatively uncatalogued relations of people in common morality is vague and can itself shift under differing conditions. Not to lie and not to commit adultery seem to be prescriptions about direct interpersonal relations of the individual. But adultery clearly concerns the institution of marriage, and lying to another violates honesty in communication that differs only in degree as it is the communication of individual to individual or communication through newspapers or radio and television. What remain uncatalogued interpersonal relations and what become institutionalized thus make no sharp difference in ethical import, except insofar as the latter pins further special responsibilities on those involved in it.[9] Indeed, moral philosophers in recent times have tended to analyze promising and similar notions as practices, and thereby suggest they differ only in degree from institutional behavior.

The point of Lincoln Steffens' view is not, therefore that institutions may reasonably do the opposite of what is prescribed in common morality but that, when the conflicts that generate the violations become endemic, it is time to reconsider the structure of the institution itself. Take, for example, the struggles of journalism with the problem of honesty. The ideal of accurate reporting calls for not only avoiding distortion but also separating editorial opinion from the news story itself. Thus, an effort at objectivity may involve presenting different points of view and relegating that of the newspaper to the editorial page. Even there an "op ed" page may attempt to present a variety of value perspectives about issues of the day, and a fairly open letter column serves in part as a complaint department. Granted that the ideal can be approached only in relative degree, it yet remains a direction of effort and incentive for fresh devices.

But suppose distortion and partiality are nevertheless endemic. Then, the whole ideal of such a newspaper may be rejected as unattainable in human affairs and productive of self-deceit. An alternative structuring would be a frank party press, as in France, in which each major sociopolitical standpoint would have its own organ, and a person who wanted an overall view would have to read several papers. Reading newspapers, then, becomes like attending a church of one's own choosing. We need not here pursue the evaluation of the different ideals; one would have to consider their impact on preparing a society to face crucial decisions, whether the danger of self-enclosed communities within one society is greater or less than that of a one-sided common ideology, how far social affairs are unavoidably subject to one-sidedness, and the like.

Many more of our institutions than we ordinarily assume are subject to basic restructuring. That an institution normally has to resolve its inner conflicts in such a way as to standardize violations of common morality is a significant index of the need for restructuring. In our changing world this has doubtless become apparent. It is not an argument for provincial moralities. That the central issue is the inner conflicts of institutions or professions in the pursuit of their aims under existent conditions can be seen if we glance at the kinds of ethical codes they tend to set up. Let me start back a bit more than half a century, dipping into Edgar L. Heermance's *Codes of Ethics: A Handbook* (1924). The Greeters of America pledge to act as God-fearing men and consecrate themselves to a love and devotion to the flag; they will be brothers of mankind and cooperate with instead of agitate against their employers.[10] The Southwestern Ice Manufacturers' Association will follow the Golden Rule in business and, recognizing the evil of giving short weight, they pay special attention to honesty in weights.[11] The Oklahoma Ice Manufacturers' Association has a more detailed code in which it includes relations to competitors. They will abstain from making disparaging statements about competitors or circulating false rumors. And they will do their part in alleviating the lot of the poor by seeing they do not suffer from want of ice—a lesson, we may add, that contemporary utilities might well observe.[12]

The canons of ethics of the American Bar Association are already detailed in 1908, for the lawyers have had a long experience. For example, the lawyer should maintain a respectful attitude to the courts as an institution, not to the specific incumbent, and he should do his best for an indigent prisoner.[13] Conflicts among lawyers are dealt with, relations to clients, fixing fees, and hosts of details. For example, a lawyer ought not to offer evidence he knows the court should reject, in order to get it before the jury by means of an argument for its admissibility.[14] By comparison, the recent Draft of Model Rules of Professional Conduct, to be acted upon by the Bar Association after several years' consideration, is much more detailed. The complexity of provisions reflects the altered character of legal practice in our contemporary world. Questions of confidentiality involve more issues of conflict; corporations as

clients have their special problems; and so on. But the major interests of
the profession, the needs to assure a respect for the system and the collection of fees, remain stable points. The treatment of misconduct is
somewhat more prominent.

In sum, the ethical codes governing different professions and enterprises are not each a self-enclosed ethics. They are reflective attempts to
see how the practitioners can achieve the aims of their enterprises and
their personal aims in pursuing the enterprises under the constraints of
common morality, within the lessons that experience has furnished for
the prevailing conditions of the time. The conditions play a constitutive
part: no medical admirer of the Hippocratic oath will feel called upon
today to teach medicine without payment to the children of his or her
teachers, nor have any past physicians faced the problems of organ
transplant and the different actions prompted by different definitions of
death. It follows that the different provincial ethics are not Applied Ethics in any distinctive sense; the application here is of the same type as
applying common morality in any individual conduct. How this latter is
to be done now constitutes perhaps our most difficult and serious issue
for the nature of morality becomes therein involved.

MORALITY APPLIED TO PARTICULAR SITUATIONS

The problems inherent in applying an established morality to particular situations of practice are perhaps more commonly recognized than
the application discussed in the two previous parts. The elements in the
morality that are applied are usually rules, principles, ideals, and vener-
ated models of character.[15] Let us illustrate from rules and principles, for
morality in our cultural tradition is largely jural and the lessons that are
drawn from their examination are easily extended to ideals and character-
models.

The process of applying rules of an established morality to particular
situations (or classes of situations) is often still regarded as a logical
one, with the rule serving as a major premise, the identification of the
particular case under the rule as a minor premise, and the decision as a
logical conclusion. "Lying is wrong; to tell you what I know (or believe)
not to be the case is lying; therefore it is wrong." This perspective of
what goes on in application focuses on the inference (recall the long
history of the deductive model in the philosophy of science), not on the

preparatory work in each unique situation that makes this inference eventually possible.

What is this preparatory work? Perhaps a useful way to see what is going on here is to take a notorious instance in the history of ethics of the attempt at a simple application of the principle of truth-telling. Consider Kant's little essay entitled "On a Supposed Right to Tell Lies from Benevolent Motives." Kant is replying to Benjamin Constant who had criticized him for asserting that "to tell a falsehood to a murderer who asked us whether our friend, of whom he was in pursuit, had not taken refuge in our house, would be a crime." [16] Kant undertakes to defend his assertion. What may strike the reader as strange is that Kant focuses directly on the one moral rule and does not explore the conflict with other obligations such as to try to save a life. Kant allows the alternative of refusing to answer, but in many situations this would be equivalent to giving an answer. Hastings Rashdall goes so far as to assert that under British law if Kant answered truthfully he would be acting as an accessory to the murder before the fact!

What complicates the situation is that it has first to be structured as a moral problem of truth-telling. Why was it faced as to lie or not to lie? In studying the ethics of the Navaho Indians, John Ladd used this example of Kant's to test for their response about telling the truth. He depicted the situation graphically as the would-be murderer holding a gun and looking for the intended victim whom the Navaho informant is supposed to have hidden. The question is the Kantian one and Ladd asked the informant, "What would you say?" The Navaho replied that he would argue with the man and remind him of previous cases where a person landed in jail for murder. Finally, to get a definite answer, Ladd had the pursuer demand he be told or else he would shoot the Navaho. Ladd asked, "What would you do then?" To which the reply was something like "Well, I'd have no choice." And just as Ladd thought that at last he would have an answer on the question of truth-telling, the informant went on: "I'd take his gun away." At no point was the problem structured as to lie or not to lie. [17]

Kant's actual defense in the little essay shows us what lies behind the stern universality on which he insists. And it is a complicated picture, not a simple logical subsumption. He says that if any untoward consequences follow from your lie in the effort to save the man's life, no matter how well intentioned you are, you are responsible for them; whereas if you have told the truth any such consequences are not your fault. If you lied by saying the person sought was not in the house when you thought he was, but had really left it, you would be responsible for his death if the murderer then caught him outside; in that case, if you had told the truth, the murderer would have been delayed looking for the man in the house! Kant clearly assumes the utter unreliability of natural events and so insists that internal purity can be maintained only by a strict adherence to the law. His ethics has no room for taking risks for moral purposes, which might bring strong feelings of unavoidable guilt.[18] It should be remembered that Kant is not holding to moral law as an external divine command where trust in God could dispel all worry about chance consequences. He is adhering to a doctrine of moral autonomy, the self-legislating for all mankind.

Moral experience surely tells against the simplistic application of moral rules or principles. Even if one tried to isolate the nest of moral values associated with truth—honesty, promise-keeping, sincerity, openness, and the rest—and hoped they could be a self-contained standard for conduct, every case of supposed application would tell a complex story. Problems are raised by not wanting to hurt others' feelings, by keeping confidences, by denying someone's right to ask a question and demand an answer, by the possibility of self-deceit, and even by the aggressive character of a complete sincerity that insists everywhere on the naked truth! The kind of application of moral law that Kant here exhibits is equivalent to abandoning any effort to come to grips with the complexity and indeterminacy in our world.[19]

What conception of moral rules would be found in an ethics that gave indeterminacy a central place, that made the moral situation not one of an internal struggle to obey the law in the face of temptation but an effort to resolve a conflict of rules and ideals and structurings of problems? Our best source for this is John Dewey's ethics. His view of the world is not a Platonic metaphysics in which the universal is the real and the particular an applied shadow of the universals. It is a complex world of change in which there is some stability and much precariousness, constant novelty. Priority lies with the particular indeterminate situation. Human achievements depend on the extent of knowledge and control, but since knowledge is at best only probable, and existence (in Santayana's picturesque phrase) "free to bloom untrammeled," any rigid fixation of the lessons of the past endangers the creative character of decision about the future.

Dewey puts the consequences of such an outlook for the nature of moral rules bluntly. As early as March 1908, shortly before the publication of the first edition of Dewey and Tufts's *Ethics*, he said in a lecture entitled "Intelligence and Morals": "There is no separate body of moral rules; no separate system of motive powers; no separate subject-matter of moral knowledge, and hence no such thing as an isolated ethical science." [20] He concludes that the business of ethics is "to converge all the instrumentalities of the social arts, law, education, economics and political science upon the construction of intelligent methods of improving the common lot." Dewey was not, of course, denying that ethics had a place for familiar codes. His wariness about them was rather that they often reflected custom and were in danger of mechanical application.

Increasingly later he drew a sharp distinction between *rules*, which for him betokened unreflective automatic compliance on the appearance of a single feature, and *principles*, which suggested aspects of the problem-situation to be explored in determining what to do. Every moral situation is one in which a reflective decision between conflicting elements has to be made. To think, therefore, in terms of a pre-existent answer issuing from an isolated set of moral truths is to cut off the creative nature of moral decision. An established morality epitomizes the lessons of past experience to be considered in analyzing present situations in the effort to determine future action. But its generalizations are to be construed as abstraction—whether in rule or principle or ideal or attachment to a model—that points in an instrumental way to an aspect of the situation deserving attention and analysis. Morality lies in the facing of problems, not in a set of formulae that replaces facing problems. Hence, an established morality is not applied to practice; it rather serves to enlighten conduct by guiding us through the exercise of intelligence.

Let us try out this conception in practice by taking what is perhaps the sharpest moral controversy of the moment—that about abortion. Note first that it is usually discussed by itself, not even in association with issues of sex education and contraception. (Of course the situation is complicated by contraception being itself controversial on grounds of some religious prohibition, and sex education is opposed by many, though in a lesser degree.) The usual form of controversy over abortion is to appeal to a selected principle that is taken to be decisive, and to make the decision about abortion a simple application of the principle. One side appeals to the principle that intentional killing is wrong (and abortion is intentional killing), the other ("prochoice") to the principle of privacy, that every woman has a right to decide about her own body and so abortion is a matter of her own choice.

Now, even on the surface, both of these principles are too strong to be applied so automatically. One can see this easily by taking other cases in which the same type of argument is likely to be rejected by those who support it in the case of abortion. It is surprising how many of the opponents of abortion are still ready to sanction war with its intentional killing or firmly defend capital punishment; if these are justified by their consequences, why not abortion even if it be seen as killing? There is, of course, the conflict about the minor premise that a fetus is a person from the beginning; defenders of abortion claim that in the early stages we have only a potential person, not an actual one, so that what potentialities are to be realized is a matter of choice.[21] The parallel metaphysical issue concerning contraception is whether the method is "natural." In both cases the metaphysical stand seems on the whole to reflect the ethical judgment, largely because the criteria for the stand prove indeterminate. A similar oversimplification holds for the prochoice principle. Few of those who defend abortion in this way would be ready to defend voluntary prostitution; or again the right to take drugs. Doubtless more would defend suicide, but on more complex grounds.

And yet, though they are both over-simplified, both principles have deep roots in the historical development of our moral culture. Both are conservative and both are deeply revolutionary. The antiabortion position is manifestly conservative in harking back to an older religious morality in conflict with secular trends and changed conditions. But its single-minded concentration on respect for life would be revolutionary if carried through all human problems, not simply used as a weapon against abortion.

While the principle of respect for life has a variable content and a complexity of problems attending its presumed application at any time, its mainstream history parallels the growth of the moral community from the time when the stranger was fair game for attack and destruction to the present effort to think in terms of the whole of humankind as one. Its particular problems are set by the material and social conditions and the extent to which humankind has been unified in fact. At present, when we are having difficulty reconciling national interests and a global perspective, respect means as a minimum live and let live, it verges on developing from philanthropy to global institutions, and it even spills over the human race to include the animal world (as in vegetarianism). And yet it struggles still with the degree to which concerted action should be taken against systematic use of torture.

In all of these cases and countless more the principle of respect for life will be invoked, but rarely as a premise from which to make deductions—rather as a profound idea that lights up whole lines of thought and feeling in reflecting on multitudes of situations. Typical actions and even institutions that we would otherwise have taken for granted suddenly become suspect. In its light, for example, "Spare the rod and spoil the child," pressed as a duty a couple of generations ago, verges on child abuse and generates an inquiry into the psychological roots of parental authoritarianism. And then as lessons are learned and feelings are transformed or developed, the institutions that embodied disrespect for life can give way.

The prochoice principle is also historically conservative because the individualism embodied in it is simply an extension of the intense individualism that our culture developed in the last three centuries. It is revolutionary in extending that individualism to women, the subjected half of the human race. That liberation movement in the twentieth century is too familiar to require recounting. One will miss the significance of the defense of abortion rights if one takes it out of that sociohistorical context. Abortion historically viewed is an unfortunately necessary instrument at the present stage of human knowledge and advancement that has to be tolerated until contraception and sexual education catch up and the creative refashioning of our institutions makes family and work conditions more congenial to the self-development of women.

A conceivable analogy for abortion would be the way in which we analyze automobile accidents—as the casualities of an institution, which one should try to minimize. In the case of automobile accidents, though journalists occasionally speak of murder on the road, society sensibly turns to driver education, to the use of education and legal compulsion against driving while drunk, to improving the roads and the cars. We do not go back to the horse and buggy in spite of the predictable body counts over every holiday weekend, because we understand the overall human gains in the place of transportation in our lives, and so we set our sights to reducing the accidents. We have generally adopted the same attitude to loss of life in what we regard as justified political revolutions. So too the losses involved in abortion are as much a part of the equalitarian revolution as sacrifices of life and the potentialities of peaceful existence are in rebellion.

Whatever line of solution a reflective moral decision about abortion today may follow, it is clearly not simply applying moral rules or principles. The principles light up avenues of insight when seen in their fuller historical scope, but the creative decision still remains to be worked out. Some, for example, may accept the permissibility of abortion as a moral compromise, seeing the effective issue as either allowing it or going back to unavoidable underground abortion mills; this compromise treats the matter in the same way as America treats alcohol and smoking, not the way it treats drugs. Others, reflecting the pluralistic character of the society and the variety of strong but variant moral convictions, decide it is an area of individual conscience. Individuals should be able to decide for themselves, or groups for their adherents. At the same time the society as a whole should take social steps through education and invention to diminish the occasions for abortion.[22] In general, a reflective solution will have to reckon with the aspects and values in all the lines of approach; they serve to enlighten conduct and decision.

Our illustration of the abortion controversy suggests that the Deweyan approach rests heavily on the assumed indeterminate element in moral problems that invites the reflective consideration of the particular as against the mere application of even established lessons; it calls for new and reconstructive formulations and solutions. This approach cannot be a priori, nor simply a postulate. It must itself be a lesson of experience over the long stretches of human history about different areas of moral problems, about the incidence of the stable and the precarious. And so it must itself be subject to the caution that there might in some areas turn out to be more stability than, in our age of transition, we have thought there would be. What we might expect, however, is that stable generalizations would be found at a high level—like the abstractions of the familiar moral codes where honesty and justice are enjoined but given different historical and circumstantial interpretations; or where stable instrumentalities are worked out in an age for furthering general ideals; or in very specialized historical situations in which the result is humanly overdetermined by strong threatened values.

Nevertheless, it is also a lesson of experience in both science and morals that we can never close the books on presumed stabilities through the confidence that seeks permanence. If the role of a general principle is primarily to show the world in a different way, to recognize what we have missed or shut out, and to prompt new directions that may guide decision and action, then refinement or even a leap to a new vista is always possible.[23] Nor can we foreclose the areas, or, for that matter, the occasions of such fresh insight. Moral principles and even moral rules, where they are not mere habits but depict conduct and attitudes about which we feel strongly, are thus ways in which conduct we contemplate is enlightened.

A genuine moral conflict is the play of different lights on different aspects of a situation that starts us on the arduous road of deliberation and decision. No one light can automatically prevail. What we have to do is to continue the enlightenment in a broadening area of our lives. To let the one light alone prevail is often to be blinded by it. The best story I have heard to make this point belongs to the 1930s when Mussolini was invading Ethiopia with the claim that Italy had to have colonies because all other great powers had colonies; he did not consider the possibility that none of them should. It took a great world war to consolidate that insight. The story is this: pious parents showed their little boy a picture of the Christian martyrs being thrown to the lions. He burst into tears. They asked why, doubtless anticipating some feeling about martyrdom. He pointed to one corner of the picture and sobbed, "This poor scrawny lion hasn't got a Christian." He was burning with the then prevalent principle of justice as fairness. Perhaps many of our present moral judgments (for example, regarding war) will eventually be seen as comparably off the mark and stuck in the groove.

If we now draw the lessons about applied ethics from all three of our studies of application—or rather from the first and third, since the second dissolved into the third—we do not find them to be different. We do not find a one-way movement from an isolated and established universal to an accommodating particular, nor do we find a simple logical relation. Nor is it formalistic verification by isolated and self-certifying intuitions. It is a matter of insight and exploration, of trying out and being satisfied with, of broadening and refining, of fresh materials brought in by connections of content or by analogy and new leads leading onward. Formal relations have their place within the whole global process, but to focus on them is to miss the reciprocal goings-on, the interplay of what in older times was called "moral experience" with moral and theoretical ideas—the interplay of principles and ideals with feelings and practices and institutions that is not the jockeying of external forces but the inner dialectic of a human life that achieves a conscious rationality.

This not-unfamiliar outcome is quite parallel to recent trends in the philosophy of science. There, too, a formalistic bias sought a precise picture of how individual theories and hypotheses were disproved or established by a set series of experiments and sensory verification to provide determinate probabilities. Important as these clarifications were, they were bought at the expense of disregarding the vast background of preponderant beliefs, guiding values, interconnection and interpenetration of theories and ideas and current and traditional structurings of

problems set before science at any time, and the wide range of interpretation within which theories could continue to be held in the face of
counterevidence. The modern shift in perspective sees the whole mass
of outlook and belief, and the historical and logical impact upon it of
growing fresh experience and articulated experiment. To construe the
process as one of enlightenment of events and experience and decision
in a matrix of belief is a profound transformation.

Perhaps we should go back to the general dictionary definition of
"application." Webster's gives "an act of putting to use," and the Latin
"applico" is to "join, connect." In that generally pragmatic sense theory is as much applied practice as practice is applied theory.

Applied Science as Model for Applied Ethics

Consider the earlier suggestion that the underlying model in Applied
Ethics may be that of Applied Science. We may therefore ask whether
Applied Science is science applied. Let us reexamine that notion, too,
in order to explore how consonant it is with our present theme.

Crudely formulated, the usual conception is that physics gives us
laws and engineering applies them to carry out our specific purposes.
But this is a much oversimplified view, even for so standard an enterprise as building a bridge. Think back on human efforts to get across
manageable bodies of water. First came fording at points where depth
permitted it, whether on foot or horse, and carrying across what men
wanted to transport. Collaterally there was swimming across. People
learned to estimate what would float and how fast a stream might thwart
their efforts. They learned to build boats and paddle or row them. At
every point the growth of knowledge in various directions enabled them
to analyze aspects of the situation and cope better with the problem of
crossing.

Then came the idea of more permanent instruments for crossing and
transporting—the idea of a bridge. Boats were moored and tied together,
or else hanging lengths of wood were chained to opposite banks, or even
supporting posts at intervals thrust into the water. People learned more
about the disrupting force of winds and currents and floods. As steel
came to be known and developed and the knowledge of corrosion and
paints and the effects of the weight and movement of traffic expanded,
and so on and on, it became possible to build the magnificent suspen-

sion structures of our contemporary world. If their construction today is regarded as applied science, the science involved is not merely physics, but chemistry, meteorology, geology, economics, and even ethics in the cooperation that makes the outcome possible. Each in its utilization is set in the known processes and traditions of the multitude of crafts that are mobilized at different points in the building process. How far is this best seen as the application of science, how far as the utilization of knowledge, some part of which comes from the various sciences and some from traditional practices and experiences? All knowledge accumulated and mobilized enlightens necessary parts of the operations of construction, and what happens to the structure in turn refines that knowledge.

The same picture can be seen in ballistics. We might loosely speak of the application of Galileo's law of falling bodies which, combined with the law of inertia, enables us to make predictions about the curved path of a projectile once a force is exerted upon it in its initial throwing. People had thrown stones and shot arrows long before Galileo's time and dropped stones from walled fortifications on the enemy below, and they had learned about the use of gunpowder in initiating the movement of objects. The least that the laws would furnish was greater precision in predicting where the projectiles would land—if people had adequate instruments for timing. The story of artillery is the same as that of bridge building. Supplementary knowledge of friction is required as well as of other distorting forces. Innumerable materials and timing devices and even the physiology of sensory reactions have to become known before we get to the degree of precision of contemporary artillery.

Even the idea of purely science-based industries is hitherto less extensive in its scope than the ordinary conception of applied science would suggest. These are the cases in which the initial phenomena are themselves the object of scientific discovery, so that their use seems to issue from the scientific knowledge itself. The history of electricity as used for human purposes would be a major example. But even here actual utilization invokes the traditional crafts that dealt with materials by which electricity is transported, the situation made humanly safe, and the product handled.

In general, studies of the history of science today no longer simply present great ideas, laws, or formulae and their establishment through ingenious experiment, and then leap to their application. There is much more attention to the whole milieu of the crafts and their growth, how they affect the instrumentation that is made available for wider uses, how new crafts grow out of the old as new instrumentation opens up fresh possibilities, how the contributions of different fields are assembled and affect one another, and what greater degrees of precision and variety become possible in newer constructions and products. [24] The general impact of such studies is not to disparage the significance of scientific law, any more than our present investigation disparages the character of moral generalizations of a high order that find a place in moral codes. It is rather to achieve a clearer idea of how they operate and what role they play in processes of human construction and processes of human moral decision.

Notes

1. For an illuminating exploration of this problem, see Oldenquist, "Rules and Consequences."

2. An excellent illustration of this outcome is the failure to protect against the consequences of working with asbestos, even after they were discovered. The Johns-Manville Company eventually resorted to bankruptcy proceedings in order to deal with problems of responsibility. For an interesting discussion of some aspects of the issue, including the Johns-Manville case, see Shue, "Exporting Hazards."

3. Bentham expected a great deal from devices of adjustment. For example, since there were delays in the payment of government workers at the time in England, he proposed a rule that the head of a government department should not receive his salary until all the workers had received theirs. Doubtless some greater sense of responsibility might be achieved today if all members of the Nuclear Regulatory Commission had to live within, say, five miles of a nuclear installation as a condition of holding their office.

4. The workers are not always on just the receiving end of such social situations. At times unions have supported the continuance of industries engaged in armament production even to a wasteful degree simply to maintain the level of employment. This can scarcely be subsumed under clean Kantian hands.

5. In Stevenson, *Ethics and Language*, ch. 2.

6. Jean Paul Sartre, "The Republic of Silence" in *The Republic of Silence*, ed. Liebling, pp. 498–500.

7. Drucker, "What is 'Business Ethics'?" p. 26.

8. For a wide ranging earlier study of the general problem, see Cabot's *Honesty*, which ranges over a number of professions. See also, Bok, *Lying*. Also, Wokutch and Carson, "Ethics and Profitability of Bluffing in Business."

9. The variability in institutionalization can be paralleled in law. For example, family law becomes a separate area in some legal systems, even with separate courts of domestic relations, while in others it is merged within the general partitions of contract, torts, and so forth.

10. Heermance, *Codes of Ethics*, pp. 237–38.

11. Ibid., p. 239.

12. Ibid., pp. 242–43.

13. Ibid., pp. 279–80.

14. Ibid., p. 285.

15. Leys has an elegant chapter on casuistry as the art of applying authoritative rules and precedents to particular present cases. He shows the parallel to law and the application of laws in decision, the need for interpretation, and the role of custom in providing security and guidance in action.

16. "On a Supposed Right to Tell Lies from Benevolent Motives" in *Kant's Critique of Practical Reason and Other Works on the Theory of Ethics*, p. 431.

17. Ladd's study of Navaho ethics is *Structure of a Moral Code*. The story is based on my recollection of his field notes, which he very kindly permitted me to read at the time.

18. The idea of unavoidable guilt is developed by Hartmann in vol. 2 of his *Ethics*. The conflict of moral values is recognized by him as a central feature of life, and to bear

the unavoidable guilt in choosing one rather than another is a mark of moral personality. Incidentally, Hartmann's complaint against a religious ethics is that it robs us of this guilt through forgiveness and so makes us less a person.

19. In fairness to Kant it should be pointed out that his major works in ethics and his *Metaphysic of Morals* (particularly in its *Theory of Virtues*) have a greater recognition of the difficulties of application.

20. Dewey, *Middle Works*, vol. 3, p. 45. 21. This is clearest in cases where abortion is used in the effort to produce a healthy child, when the parents have genetic defects and early diagnosis of the fetus is possible. If the chances of a healthy child are, say, one in three, a readiness to employ abortion in successive pregnancies is an alternative to childlessness.

22. Note how even within such a decision there will be further controversies from opposing sides. To make sure that conscience operates and is well advised, one side attempts to pass legislation making doctors give stern medical warnings and horrendous descriptions, or else insists on parents being notified in the case of minors; the other wants advisory confidential clinics and women's centers. Again, in preventive measures, the one will stress moral-religious training, the other sex education.

23. Redfield in his *Primitive World*, ch. 5, gathers illustrations of such moral leaps from dramatic and courageous individual acts that stopped traditional practices: for example, the abolition of ancient food taboos in Hawaii or of human sacrifice among the Pawnee.

24. I am indebted to Hunter Dupree for clarifying discussion of this whole process.

3

The Good Person and The Good Society:
Some Ideals, Foolish and Otherwise
Warner A. Wick

When my friends and I thought of ourselves as bright young things, we used to entertain each other with a game based on the conjugation of a verb in the present tense, but with alleged equivalents substituted for the original verb or predicate adjective, as in "I know, you believe, he (or she) fancies that . . ." Or "I am firm, you are stubborn, he is a pig-headed fool!" The point, of course, was to suggest that each verb had the same cash value, once the personal perspective was eliminated. I now offer you as if it were a play in our old game: "I am an idealist, you are sometimes overzealous, but he is a fanatic!" How does one tell an idealist from a fanatic? And is it important to distinguish kinds of idealists and ideals?

IDEALS AND FANATICISM

What I suggest here may be regarded as a corrective supplement to my Lindley Lecture at the University of Kansas in 1980, when I complained of the "meager" terms in which we have become accustomed to discuss and think about issues of public policy and personal choice. For example, I suspect that most people would be embarrassed, and expect not to be taken seriously, were they to advocate a course of action as "the honorable or noble thing to do," the alternative being "ignoble" or shameful. Instead, we are more comfortable and confident in appealing to what makes for human welfare, measured by likely success in getting what people actually want or at least in avoiding what is harmful or disagreeable.

Is this just a matter of style, like the move from ball gowns to blue jeans for parties? Anyway, talk of honor and other resplendent virtues gives many of us a creepy feeling; we see them as either quaintly anachronistic, out of touch with the utilities and preferences we have learned to accept as the rational determinants of choice, or else elitist and, therefore, viciously anachronistic because the notion of superior and inferior persons doesn't jibe with modern egalitarian sentiments. A consequence of this restriction to what is agreeable and useful is, I argued in my Lindley Lecture, "the effective disappearance of one of the three main categories of good and evil" that had always been recognized in our civilization.

In Cicero's version, for example, the three were called the *jucundum* and the *utile*—the pleasant and expedient just mentioned—and what we now seem to lack, the *honestum*, what is nobly worthy of respect and reverence but rarely if ever achieved. I noted that this impoverishment of the media of discussion brings our working conceptual arsenal into conformity with philosophical utilitarianism; and I suggested some reasons why the world has pretty generally adopted the language and attitudes of utilitarianism even while philosophers have become increasingly critical of them.

At any rate, the burden of my Lindley Lecture was to remind us of the values that we hold to be "beyond price," and which the unsophisticated morality of our world has always taken for granted. They are beyond price just because a price means a quantity of some other good or goods for which it would make sense to trade them. Therefore they can't be handled by the calculus of utilities and preferences, for that works only for values that are comparable by some common measure. But common morality says that treachery is evil in itself, not redeemable by any gains that would render its use good on the whole, while the service of some causes is so precious as to be worth dying for—that is, worth giving up the whole game of satisfying wants, whose objects are good only if somebody should want them. I concluded with some borrowed eloquence about rising above the humdrum level of the useful and agreeable to serve ideals that we conceive as being on another plane entirely. At Williams College there is an open-air granite staircase inscribed with the legend, "Climb high, climb far, your goal the sky, your aim a star." It did not say, "Satisfy as many wants as you can, at the least cost in effort and discomfort," although that is claimed to define the scope of reason in action.

But now our old parlor game suggests that one person's idealist is another's crazy fanatic. And this hypothesis gets philosophical support from R. M. Hare, the noted Oxford moralist, who has been much concerned about fanatics and fanaticism. For he identifies a fanatic as one committed to values that he excludes from comparative pricing and therefore, apparently, from the scrutiny of rational criticism. If Hare is right, the pursuit of any of Cicero's and the Western tradition's third class of goods "beyond price" is simply fanatical, so that it would be wiser to settle for the expedient, which is calculable, and the agreeable, any item of which can be outweighed by a sufficient quantity of other agreeable objects. But to do that would concede that every goal, and every man or woman who acts for any purpose, has its, his, or her price. To examine this association of ideals with fanaticism is an especially fitting project for an essay dedicated to the memory of my old friend, Wayne Leys, whose skeptical insight was unrivaled in spotting hokum.

IDEALS WITHIN MORAL PHILOSOPHY

There are some familiar distinctions among the kinds of issues about action. They should suggest where and how ideals and their possibly fanatical sponsors might make trouble. Among the areas of intelligent action there is, first, the vast territory of the productive arts or technologies, in which we apply what we have learned about causes and effects in order to make shoes and space shuttles, write piano sonatas, drain swamps, or make the desert bloom. However difficult or even impracticable it may be in particular cases to work out a procedure for producing some desired result with the resources we have, the nature of technical rationality (or rational technology) is not problematic; and neither does it, in itself, raise questions of right and wrong except in the sense of being "correct" or "incorrect." Here everything depends on the principle that if you want to achieve some X, then you must (or rather rationally "ought" to, since you don't *have* to do anything) do Y, Z, or W, for that is how X's are pulled off. So if Y, Z, or W should be unacceptable or beyond your capacities, you had better forget about X for now; while if they are merely difficult or disagreeable it is up to you to decide whether X is worth that to you.

Technical rationality, then, has its own practical canon with its strict but limited constraints, but since it is entirely a matter of ways and means it has nothing whatever to say about what ought to be done until someone gives it a job to do. And then the responsibility is its employer's. This is to say that technology has no moral significance of its own and no favorites, offering to serve any purpose whatever, no questions asked.

However, we need to coordinate our activities and the ends they serve if we are not to bog down in inner tangles, and, since we cannot live human lives in isolation, to coordinate our activities and aims with those of other people. So we need principles of wider scope and less conditional authority than the canon of technology; and this introduces the topics of moral philosophy proper.

For our purposes it will be convenient to follow the eighteenth century practice of distinguishing two main divisions of the moral. The first is that of justice under law, with rights and duties specifying minimal constraints that must be observed in the "external" arena of common life if our unregulated pursuits are not to collide in strife and insecurity. For although we humans are "social animals" who depend on each other to survive and flourish, we are equally notable for our "antisocial" readiness to push each other around in the scramble to satisfy our wants. This duality, which Kant called man's "unsocial sociability," is an inescapable feature of the human condition; and it has much to do with the difference between benign and foolish ideals that I will be exploring.

The second part of morals concerns the "internal" or "ethical" aspects of action (from *ethos*: character, disposition), such as the merit of one's intentions and our reasons for doing as we do. This part is needed to clarify what is wrong with the Pharisee, who makes a fetish of the letter of the law but washes his hands of any further responsibility; and the scoundrel who challenges us to catch him in anything illegal, all the while scheming to subvert the spirit of justice through some loophole in the statutes. Ethics, as a doctrine of virtues and ends, rounds out the picture of the moral world.

The principle of justice as a semiautonomous part of morals calls for limiting each person's freedom just to the extent necessary to make its use consistent with the equal freedom of all according to rules acknowledged to apply to everyone alike. If that sounds negative, I can put the same point positively: justice guarantees to all the same freedom to do whatever does not encroach upon the equal freedom of others. This principle is "formal" in the sense that it purports to hold for all possible legal systems, which may vary indefinitely in detail, adherence to the principle being the criterion of their legitimacy, just as a formal principle of inference holds for all possible arguments having a certain form, which is the standard measuring their validity. The principle is "formal" in a second sense, too, in that it pays no attention to differences in merit among individuals and their particular reasons for paying their debts, making good their promises, or refraining from stealing and fraud.

That the legality of action consists only in its conformity to valid law, regardless of one's intentions in doing so, is the reason why the figure of Justice, personified in stone in front of a court house, is usually blindfolded as she holds her scales; and it is also why St. Thomas More, as lord chancellor of England, could proudly declare that he would uphold the right of the Devil to live unmolested in London so long as he conformed to English law. Moreover, it is precisely because external conformity is sufficient to satisfy the demands of law that it is possible to enforce justice by the coercive power of government, its rewards and punishments inducing compliance among those who would not conform through an ethical respect for justice itself. As the Declaration of Independence says, it is "to secure these rights that governments are instituted among men."

But the possibility—indeed the practical necessity—of enforcing legal justice should not beguile anyone into thinking that the rule of law is ultimately only a matter of power. The principle to which I have been appealing is inherently normative, formulating the measure and limits of legitimacy in the exercise of power. According to this strict standard there are plenty of governments with scarcely a shadow of legitimacy, while in substantially legitimate ones like our own not every official command backed by power qualifies as having the authority of law. And of course, man's unsocial sociability being what it is, every society has not only bullies and gangs of thieves but many putatively respectable centers of organized power that extort advantages for themselves in violation of the equal liberty of justice. It is to mitigate and redress such recurrent, and to some extent inevitable, wrongs that we have courts of civil and constitutional jurisdiction in which both private agencies and public officials can be brought to book when they overstep the limits of legality.

Here, then, we have encountered our first full-fledged social ideal, generated by the principle of justice, which, as I said, is inherently normative. This ideal of justice under law would seem to be at least a part of anyone's idea of a good society, as a necessary foundation for any embellishments one might wish to add. And it is without question an ideal—"only" an ideal if you like, for it has never been fully realized on

earth and, I should argue, never can be. I will defer my reasons for saying that, as well as my examination of justice's credentials as a good
beyond price, and of whether, if sought as such, it qualifies its seekers
as fanatics. Instead, we should notice that this mention of commitment
to justice as an ideal has brought us, perhaps unexpectedly, within the
scope of the second, "ethical" part of morals in general; and since it
has, it would be better to outline an account of that part and its relation
to the doctrine of justice and rights.

That the ideal of justice falls within the ethical domain, even though
it is "of" justice and its external legalities, follows from its being an end
to be aimed at; for the ends we pursue, whether ideal or mundane, are,
like any other reasons for which a person acts, *necessarily* a matter of
internal self-determination. This may sound like strange doctrine, even
heresy, in an age notorious for manipulating opinion and patterns of
mass consumption. For does not the manipulation of behavior work by
controlling the reasons why people act? No, not exactly. What is con-
trollable is never a reason for action until somebody freely makes it one.
It is true that our wants can be stimulated, extended, even "created,"
and that the conditions of satisfying them can be altered by arranging
the circumstances in which a person acts. It is also true that most—not
all—of our practical objectives are selected from the things we want,
and that most people, most of the time, choose according to their perceived interests, "maximizing their utility functions" as the behavioral
scientists say. But the fact that we want something does not necessarily
become an effective reason for doing anything about it. We all have
countless wants and wishes that never lead to any action at all. The
things we want become actual ends-in-view only by being made so
through our choices, which are our own from first to last.

To illustrate this all-important point, and also to understand better the
relation between justice as an ethical ideal determining individual
choices and justice as a more or less enforceable legal order, let us di-
gress briefly to think again about enforcing obedience. Let us agree that
we have a general *ethical* obligation to obey any valid law, but ethical
only because we respect its moral authority. Because of this the ethical
point of view encompasses and adopts the domain of law, adding internal ethical commitment to externally enforceable legal duties.

But now suppose I don't see the justice of some accepted legal rule, or
even regard the whole business of so-called justice as a cynical imposition of the powerful upon the weak? What can organized society, armed
with its dominations and powers, do about me? What it *cannot* do is

impel me to respect its justice and enlist my commitment. The most it can do is to "make it worth my while" to conform, assuming—in most cases correctly—that I wish to avoid the hassles it is prepared to visit upon me if I refuse.

Given the alternatives, I may or may not choose to submit, but in either case it will be for *my* reasons and in pursuit of *my* objectives. Should I choose to comply in order to get the authorities off my back, I "obey," not the law, but my own imperative of prudence after estimating my chances with the enforcers. That is the only way law can be "enforced"—as external conformity, not as ethical obligation, which each person must freely accept. But I may choose to risk all, even my life, rather than submit to what I believe is unjust. It happens every day. It is a commonplace that governments lacking respect for their authority are never secure. Consider the example of Poland. It is not so often recognized that this is because reasons for action are necessarily each person's own, though they may be shared.

This digression has, I hope, been persuasive in arguing that autonomous choice entails and is entailed by a characteristic feature of all ethically significant action: that it must be for the sake of some end respected as ideal—"because it is the right thing to do," and therefore beyond price in comparison with agreeable and useful alternatives. While many, perhaps most people, conform to standards of legality by following the path of least resistance—"resistance" being gauged in terms of expected disagreeableness—they may therefore support justice by indirection, for ethically irrelevant reasons. It is fortunate for society that they do so support it, but their actions remain without ethical merit: they are not what moral agents ideally ought to be; they are without virtue, and they act as if virtue were not important to them.

All this follows if we grant, first, the crucial difference between doing something because it is right and doing it because it pays (although much that pays is also right and vice versa), and if, second, human agents are capable of acting for ethically significant reasons even when their "druthers" incline them in the opposite direction. It is this capacity that I hope my digression has made acceptable. The former premise I take as simply undeniable if moral philosophy in both its parts is not reducible to technology, the art of getting whatever one wants, provided that one could control the necessary conditions.

However, before I abandon this account of the topics of morals as background for assessing the relation of moral ideals to fanaticism, I must finish the outline of its ethical part. If ethically significant actions are confined to what we do from regard for the right and because failure to do so would be, if not undesirable in most ways, somehow shameful, incompatible with one's self-respect, then there is something reflexively self-regarding in all moral excellence, however "selfless." This is because moral merit comes from the ethical quality of one's character as an agent, comprising one's aim, the constraints one observes in the choice of means, and one's incentive in fixing upon both: was it regard for the right and honorable way, or was it secretly self-serving in some pejorative sense? As Socrates insisted, care for our own souls must come first, which is not the same as care for our comfort and convenience. In other words, the only excellence that we can be responsible for is our own, so that the ideal of virtue or self-perfection is a necessary ingredient in all ethical motivation and is thus a heading for a variety of specific virtues and for an essential aspect of all the rest.

Lest one be bemused by habits of thinking of "the moral point of view" as primarily concerned with the other fellow's good and shrink from me as a perverse egoist, I hasten to correct any such impression. Think again of justice. We have encountered it first and primarily as an ideal order of society, yet demanding personal commitment, and secondly as a more or less enforceable system of laws and sanctions implementing that ideal. But justice is also recognized as a personal virtue, the self-directed disposition to act with respect for the equal liberty and dignity of all. Like all virtues, justice is an element of the ideal person, of what the ethical duty of self-perfection would have us achieve, even though it can be made actual only in our treatment of, and attitude toward, others. What, then, is strange about acknowledging that in treating others as we ought we also improve ourselves, and the other way around?

But are there not other ethical duties regarding others besides those exhibited in the virtue of justice? The ideal community would be a community of ideal persons too, wouldn't it—the "community of saints" in the language of religion? Ought we then to try to improve our neighbor's characters? Here we must be careful. Recall the argument that the ethical significance of action is wholly a matter of the agent's "internal" reasons for doing as he or she does, so that it is impossible to "make people good" by the pressures of law or public opinion. We can only induce them to go through the appropriate motions for their own reasons, be the reasons admirable or not. The consequence is that we can do nothing directly to improve other people's morals. That they must do for themselves just because the only virtues anyone *can* be responsible for are his or her own.

However this does not mean that there is nothing at all to be done for other people beyond respecting their rights, especially their right to pursue happiness and virtue on their own, free from officious meddling like "It's for your own good, you know." In addition to observing the negative restraints of justice, we can give positive help—that is, make others' legitimate ends our own—not by acting in their places but by generously making available means and opportunities. This amounts to promoting benevolently human welfare, welfare meaning the relative control people have over the conditions and equipment for achieving their goals. But it is worth remembering that some of the most important of such conditions are competences like health and knowledge, which are not themselves transferable. We humans stubbornly resemble the horse who can be led to water but can't be made to drink. The beneficiaries of our goodwill can't remain wholly passive if they are to benefit from it.

So now we have three summary categories of ideals, all intricately but compatibly linked together so as to constitute the comprehensive ideal of an ethical community of the free enjoying mutually sustained levels of welfare. These ideal categories generate ethical duties of justice, of goodwill toward others, and of care for one's own moral integrity and virtue. Their regular observance gives rise to associated virtues that, taken together, constitute the ideal person. We have already noticed that to call these distinct types of duties, and distinct virtues, for purposes of exposition and analysis does not mean that the very same *action* may not satisfy all of them at once. For example, every ethically benevolent act must meet the ethical demands of justice as well, and in doing so it confirms and strengthens the agent's virtue.

Justice, however, a "formal" ideal as I have explicated it, is distinctive in that, though an ideal, its associated duties are definite and limited in scope. Thus justice requires that I repay your thousand-dollar loan in ninety days, plus twelve percent interest, but no more, for that was our contract. You have no further rights in that transaction. Justice entails no concern of mine to care for your welfare, although the virtue of justice does require that I give you your due in the ethical spirit of respect for the right and for you as a person having rights.

In contrast, both the self-regarding duties and virtues and those of goodwill toward others are indefinite and open-ended—in one respect less strict but in another far more demanding. They are less strict in not specifying how and in what degree I ought to develop my virtues and work for the welfare of my neighbors and others more remote. They are more demanding in that I can never say, "There, at last I have done enough" and bask in self-congratulation, whereas I can with good conscience tell a creditor or tax collector that he has had his just deserts and should stop badgering me with further talk of his rights.

FANATICISM: PATHOLOGICAL COMMITMENT TO IDEALS

I have now outlined—perhaps tediously—a supposedly coherent conception of the structure and elements of the moral world that was articulated some two hundred years ago by several thinkers and is reasonably in tune with the shared moral convictions of Western civilization. It has also been the basis of the liberal political tradition embodied in the Declaration of Independence and in the rationale of the United States Constitution formulated in the *Federalist Papers*. My purpose has been to provide a not unfamiliar context in which to consider my opening question about goods not measurable by utilities relative to wants taken simply as "given"—these being the stock in trade of philosophical utilitarianism, welfare economics, and what is called social choice theory. Do such ideal goods, literally "beyond compare," open the way to fanaticism, dangerous because, in addition to being allegedly impervious to argument, fanatics accept no restraints upon the pursuit of their often high-minded schemes?

Well, my exposition has not been lacking in appeal to ideal ends as the objects of rights, duties, and virtues; and it should be sufficiently evident that all of them are off the scale of comparable preferences and utilities. That the principle of justice is not derivable from the apparatus of utilitarianism, despite the valiant efforts of John Stuart Mill, has become generally conceded in these days of John Rawls, Robert Nozick, and others. Their rival treatments of justice recognize it as setting rational constraints within which the pursuit of happiness and utility must be confined; and as conceptually prior to and restrictive of the calculus of comparative values, justice is clearly not conceived as but one more interest among those whose values are being compared and summed.

Again, the ideal of personal excellence, commitment to which I have represented as the mark distinguishing the morality of action from its external conformity and technical efficiency, is clearly both an imperfectly realizable ideal and beyond pricing on the scale of interests. Moreover, since the ideal person's respect for his own virtue entails commitment to promoting the welfare of others equally with his own, and to the self-restraints of justice in respecting everyone's freedom and integrity as he does so, it sums up all the subdivisions of morals from the agent's point of view. But it is only the agent's perspective that makes potential ends, ideal or not, actually ends of action; and as I argued above, morally significant action must be for the sake of some end respected as ideal rather than as the object of a given want. In morals, we may say, ideals are the name of the game.

Should we not, then, understand fanaticism more narrowly—perhaps as a certain pathology of the commitment to ideals? Let us explore this possibility after first asking whether the ideals I have been talking about lend themselves to perversion. Notice the safeguards built into my outline. Moral ideals have been represented as objectives of ethical *self-determination*. The idealist who pledges his all to the cultivation of (his) virtue is not much tempted to harm anyone, besides which his commitment requires him to care for his neighbor as for himself, while respecting the latter's equal liberty to set his own course within the law. He does not, and cannot, pledge other people's lives and fortunes to his cause. At worst such an idealist may appear as a somewhat Quixotic figure, harmlessly charming in his gallantry. Where most of us fall short is in aiming too low, whereas he neglects everyday enjoyments and conveniences for the sake of his dream.

How, then, might fanaticism in commitment to ideals arise? The decisive point is passed, I suggest, when one oversteps the limits set by the equal liberty and dignity of every human agent. This typically occurs when enthusiasm for some notion of an ideal society, not anchored in the "merely formal" conditions of justice, is impatient with the constraints of the latter: in effect failing to recognize the mutual interconnections of the ideals that make up the moral perspective. Illustrations from the religious persecutions that prompted the development of the liberal tradition are easy for us to understand, lacking sympathy as we do for the particular enthusiasms that caused the trouble. Thus it is one thing to urge, as Lincoln did, that we have "confidence in the right as God gives us to see the right," modestly acknowledging that God alone is all-seeing; it is quite another to assume that our understanding of God's will has final authority, sanctioning all measures necessary to root out the Devil's influence. The latter stance, in the language of religion, is at once blasphemous in frivolously claiming the name and authority of God for mere human judgment, and idolatrous in worshiping a graven image—that is, one's own image of divine things.

All this may seem obvious and of little relevance to what we nowadays regard as serious issues. So let us shift attention to the reasons why the liberal tradition of former days has been getting a bad press. A principal objection has been directed at its "merely formal" and libertarian conception of justice and rights, in which the equality of justice is restricted to equality before the law, and rights are enforceable guarantees of liberty and security in one's person and possessions against invasion by private individuals and groups or by the state. Accordingly, recent discussions of justice have focused instead upon the fair distribution of benefits and burdens: does justice call for equal shares of both, or does it ask "from each according to his ability" and give "to each according to his need"—or alternatively, according to his actual contribution, to his merit, or to whatever?

In any case some agency must fix the measure of equality, need, merit, and so forth, as well as cut and distribute the pie. Unlike the justice of the older liberalism, which made no distinctions among persons save as to the legality of their behavior and was otherwise "blind," the new variety must be all-wise in order to determine desert correctly, and all-powerful if it is to execute its judgments. There has been a corresponding transformation in the notion of rights, which has added substantive entitlements to what is due to anyone according to some particular rule of distributive justice—for example, the so-called "welfare rights" to a job, to paid vacations, to a healthful diet, and so on. And again, these rights can not be made effective by individuals who respect generally intelligible criteria and can act accordingly on their own, but need some central authority to make the requisite benefits available and allocate them according to its determination of "fair shares."

The first consequence of these shifts is to magnify the powers and responsibilities of government enormously, for it must decide and allocate as well as produce any extra goods that may be necessary. Government becomes the "mortal god" Hobbes spoke of: mortal because it can be overthrown; a god, however, in overwhelming power but not in omniscience or goodness.

A second consequence is that all issues of social organization become—to use a mild term—politicized. Everything turns on government's division of the pie, and therefore upon who controls the determination of "who gets what, when, and how." As in high school basketball, competition for control of the floor whips up passions, leading to extremes—fanaticism. Endless strife is the inevitable result, its most disagreeable features mitigated only where there are enough different contending parties to prevent any one from having its way, so that an unstable immobility can imitate peace.

A third, more fundamental consequence is erosion of respect for the equal liberty and dignity of humankind. Of course everybody values their own freedom—which is not to say that everybody values everybody's freedom. The trouble is that the recalcitrance of "others" is seen to stand in the way of realizing our notions of a better order of things, generously conceived as they may be. According to the imperative of technical rationality, if a desired state of things is to be realized, it is necessary to control the conditions of bringing it about—in this case, control over the behavior of everyone needed to carry out the plan worked out by masters of the appropriate technical expertise.

But control means power, which must be used if the plan is not to be given up. So when problems arise, the perceived remedy is to demand that the government make some supposed laggard or obstructionist shape up. Modern liberalism thus suffers from a grievous internal conflict: its underlying motivation is a wish to believe in the dignity and perfectibility of every human soul, yet the means it adopts treat citizens as instruments to be manipulated for their several benefits and for the common good. But that is demeaning, and makes for resentment and envy of the masters. Who can be more unequal in freedom and respect than the one who gives directions and one whose role is to be directed?

These gloomy observations are confirmed by experience. The history of revolutions, beginning with the French, has been the story of a slide from the exhilaration of Bastille Day, with its vision of liberty, equality, and fraternity, to a reign of terror. Though the goal is to elevate the downtrodden, the intended beneficiaries are found to be hard to organize efficiently, either because they haven't the needed skills, lack enthusiasm for discipline amid promises of liberty, or are even hostile as a result of "false consciousness." So an elite vanguard, skilled, disciplined and loyal, takes over the revolution—in short, the Party as custodian of the people, kept alert by a series of internal purges and secure by maintaining a network of informers and spies as zealously watchful, and corruptible, as the agents of the Inquisition. To be sure, this is envisaged as a temporary period of transition, regrettably necessary, since you can't make an omelette without breaking some eggs. Eventually— or so it is said with fading conviction as the gulags persist—the day will come when the state itself will have withered away.

A second source of social fanaticism is illustrated in this faith that tyrannical measures need be only a passing stage in the realization of the ideal. This belief in the transience of tyranny has many forms, but they all share one basic confusion—I should call it a metaphysical confusion—between the ideal and what is achievable in human experience, as if the Heavenly Kingdom could be instituted on earth if only certain corrupting agencies were wiped out. What I venture to call the Marxist theology is the most common current form of it.

Thus it is assumed that human wants are finite, so that the earth's bounty, though also finite, is sufficient to satisfy everyone were it not wastefully misappropriated through the exploitation of man by man. History is the process through which the prisoners of starvation are oppressed by a succession of ruling classes, controlling each evolving method of organizing labor's productivity and skimming off surplus value for themselves; and states, with their successive versions of so-called "justice," are the institutional mechanisms of this class domination as well as the agents of imperialism and war. Meanwhile the exploited become alienated from their labor and from each other, thereby increasing man's inhumanity to man.

However, "come the revolution," all of this shall pass away. Classes will disappear as the means of production are socialized, and with them all the sources of domination and corruption, including the state itself. This withering away of the state will mark the end of history and war, and the birth of a new epoch of freedom, peace, brotherhood, plenty, and every other blessing; for without the social causes of corruption, the natural goodness of human nature will flower. Isn't all this worth some transitional terror, especially as this scenario is the necessary outcome of objective historical forces for which no one can be held responsible anyway? The most graphic description of this vision is found in two passages in the Book of Isaiah—with the essential difference that Isaiah's prophecy was to be effected by God's grace, not by human agency: "The wolf also shall dwell with the lamb, and the leopard shall lie down with the kid; and the calf and the young lion and the fatling together" (11:6). "And [people] shall beat their swords into plowshares, and their spears into pruninghooks: nation shall not lift up sword against nation, neither shall they learn war any more" (Is 2:6).

In contrast to this, the liberals of the Enlightenment have been reproached for their jaundiced, even cynical, estimate of human nature. I have mentioned Kant's hard-nosed observation of man's natural "unsocial sociability." Like the parties in a rocky marriage, we can't live apart, yet neither can we live together in harmony without the rule of law, maintained by the enforcing power of civil government, which is fortunately capable of being guided by the rational ideal of justice. As Kant added in his famous essay, *Toward Perpetual Peace*, it is only as the human race becomes, literally *civil*ized under the rule of law that there is an opportunity for many to "get the idea" of ethical commitment to justice and the duties of virtue.

David Hume makes the same points in a somewhat different way. Human avarice for acquiring goods and possessions is perennial, insatiable, and universal. It cannot be controlled by another passion but rather only by radically altering its direction through the "artifical" system of justice. To it we have what he calls a "natural obligation," meaning that apart from simple "folly," everyone can see that while individual acts of justice may be opposed to private or public interest, the whole scheme of justice is indispensable for the continued existence of society and the well-being of each of its constituent individuals—even of the ones who take advantage of opportunities to cheat. Legal sanctions only reinforce this natural obligation.

In addition, as for Kant, there is a supervening "moral obligation" based on an appreciation of the difference between right and wrong, the honorable and dishonorable, as the basis of self-respect. But neither Hume nor Kant thought it anything but foolishness to look forward to the establishment of a human community whose members would not be "all too human," subject to "the old Adam" in us all. The experience of the twentieth century has reminded us that the veneer of civilization is very thin.

It was in this same frame of mind that James Madison and his fellow Federalists designed the United States Constitution so that its success would not depend upon the fantasy of some patriots that the executors of its various powers, and the citizens who elected them, would be blessed with more virtue or wisdom than the next man, or that under the new regime men and women would be motivated differently than history records the peoples of other nations as having always been.

It may be admitted nowadays that human nature was not created all at once, so that it is no doubt continuing to evolve. It is possible that it may move in a welcome direction. But not so fast that you would notice it. And you had better not count on it!

To sum up a bit too crudely, ideals are an essential feature of ethical motivation, which gives action its moral significance through self-commitment. It would be perverse to call someone a fanatic in the demands that person makes only upon himself or herself. An ideal for other people to conform to, if pressed upon them beyond the limits of reciprocal respect required by justice—itself an ideal—would be fanatical in its obsession with one overriding value, but not because it accepted an ideal not relative to given interests. And "idealism" that disregards human experience and the limited perfectibility of human nature is simple foolishness. The ideal community is "not of this world."

4

Public Benefit, Private Costs
John Lachs

A BROKEN AND AN INTEGRATED WORLD

We live in a broken world and know not how to mend it. People down-town approach in fear; neighbors view each other with suspicion. Parents see their children as strangers in the house and we are isolated in human company. The sources of power are hidden from almost everyone and we feel drawn to symbolic, defiant, single acts. The daily life of the nation appears to consist of disconnected events without purpose and lasting issue. No one understands how our efforts unite to make a greater whole and why our best hopes are abandoned or else dashed. In prior years the times may have been out of joint; today they appear utterly dismembered.

We also live in a tightly unified world we are anxious to escape. In our jobs and as members of the state, we are stapled to each other and a common fate. Our movements are monitored and regulations govern our acts. Others control what we can do, where we must yield, what we must give. Narrow roles in gigantic institutions define us; we are hemmed in on all sides. We march or stumble through a crowded world contributing to acts we never see, helping to cause effects none fully wants or knows. The thought of privacy and hope for self-determination haunt us because their reality is unattainable.

The broken world and the tight crowded world are organically connected. Understanding their relation is indispensable for learning what ails us and for therapy. Yet we have made remarkably little headway in the last several hundred years in giving a sensible and unified account of the concurrent growth of fragmentation and integration in society. At least one part of the reason for this is the interest in remediation. Social problems tend to be the province of social reformers, and those who wish to bring about change must identify a relatively simple and eliminatable cause of our distress. If the problems of social life are the diffuse costs of living in a complex and populous world, for example, improvement in our condition may appear elusive or impossible. The reformer, therefore, naturally seeks a special cause and a unique malfunction: ridding ourselves of this one difficulty promises a resolution of all our problems. Analysis of alienation-phenomena has suffered from this simplistic approach, which has sometimes been disguised by technical language and theoretical embellishments, from Rousseau to Marcuse.

What tends to stand behind the fervor for change is a vision of how things ought to be. This ideal introduces a powerful value bias into what should be a cool description of the bewildering, and perhaps irreducible, variety of social causes and effects. The dispassionate examination of how well our views fit the facts is then replaced by the search for evidence to support our ideas. Frequently, alienation-theorists appear to work by a reverse procedure: they identify the source of our problems as whatever stands in the way of their favorite utopia, instead of recommending cautious ameliorative steps on the basis of a tentative, empirically responsible account of our situation.

I have no vision to offer of what would be good for everyone. And, though I am by no means uninterested in improving our lot, I firmly believe that a measure of understanding must precede any work for social change. This understanding is not likely to be advanced by theories that attempt to identify supposed special malfunctions, such as the private ownership of the means of production or the breakdown of traditional community values. Our chance for progress in this field will be vastly enhanced if we try to see social problems as natural attendants of social life. Rain makes the flowers grow but also gets us wet; it is perfectly natural, though not logically necessary, that this be so. Similarly, it is best to start with the supposition that social arrangements have both costs and benefits, and that these hang together in some natural, intelligible way. The philosopher's job is to formulate a theory that elucidates this connection. The point is to reduce the diversity of facts to the unity provided by a few concepts. These ideas cannot, of course, be expected to explain everything. But their value is proportional to the breadth of the phenomena on which, by interconnecting them, they manage to shed some light. The theory I shall propose is exactly of this sort. I am glad for it to be judged by the measure of improvement it provides in our current grasp of the way in which the benefits of social life are accompanied in the course of things by certain pervasive costs. Let me begin with a mode of thought natural to the broken world. Analysis into atomic constituents or isolated factors yields excellent results in science. The sequence of happenings in daily life may seem continuous, yet we think it is a flow of discrete, minuscule events. For there are potential turning points everywhere; if only I had not slammed on the brakes when I hit that patch of ice, if only Othello had not believed Iago, if only Nixon had not recorded his conversations, or the recordings had not been discovered, or if at least he had not erased them, everything would be different. In this way, we convince ourselves that our actions have crisis points, small segments or atomic units that constitute their heart.

This tends to make us lose all sense of the unity or continuity of our acts. In fact, of course, intention insensibly flows into the early stages of what we know as physical act and guides its performance throughout. Consequence also is ubiquitous: the act is outcome of the intention and consists of complex parts, the later of which are at least partly results of the earlier. Distant intention and consequences thus define our physical acts. An action, in the full sense of the word, is in fact a unity of intention, physical performance, and consequences. Like the flight of the boomerang, it is an unbroken process; we can distinguish its parts but it is artificial to declare one its isolated heart and wrong to identify any with the whole.

COMPLETE ACTIONS

In ideally complete or at least maximally intelligible actions, the intention, physical act, and attendant consequences all reside in a single agent. Noting my hunger, intending to relieve it, raiding the refrigerator, fixing a sandwich, eating it, and experiencing the pleasures of taste and then of satiation, is a continuous process; in it I know in a most real, immediate way what it means to do something, what is done, why I do it, and what it takes to bring it about. It is this notion of the individually initiated, performed, and enjoyed (or suffered) act that serves as the generating ideal of human freedom. In autonomous actions desires lead to intentions and we are able to perform what we intend. Those, like John Stuart Mill, who have not embraced metaphysical obscurities in

their account of freedom, have always known that it consists of the coin-
cidence of desire and ability to act in a single person. In order to achieve
self-determination, we must want or welcome what we do and, in turn,
do what we desire. Thinking of it in this way immediately reveals the
natural connection of freedom and responsibility. For liberty consists of
the continuity or unity of intention and physical act. Responsibility, by
contrast, is the undivided oneness of what we do and of the consequences which flow from it. Freedom is lodged in the first phase of a
completed action, in the process of converting plan into execution. Responsibility resides in the second phase and consists of the way our action changes the world, of the consequences we must learn to bear as a
result of what we did. So long as intention, physical act and outcome
are all centered in the agent, freedom and responsibility remain insep-
arable realities.

In the broken world, however, the single-agent unity of actions is destroyed. Much of what I do fails to achieve the dignity of a full action,
namely, one which I plan and execute, and whose consequences I bear.
In much of our lives we have become participants in larger social acts,
and in these each of us plays but a minor role. A social act, such as the
provision of air service between cities, defines multiple contributory
roles. Many individuals provide for its possibility, sometimes without
knowing that they do so, by making metal and plastic parts or by assem-
bling planes, by calling in weather data or by refining oil. A relatively
few, the presidents of corporations, schedulers, and financial analysts,
serve as planners. A large number, such as pilots, mechanics, and bag-
gage handlers, share the burden of actually providing the service.
Others, ranging from the customers who fly to those deafened when the
planes take off, enjoy or suffer the consequences.

The Integrated but Dismembered Social Act

In one sense, then, the social act is dismembered. Intending, doing
and dealing with the consequences become separate affairs occupying
individuals at a physical and psychological remove from one another.
And each of these main functions is itself divided into innumerably
minute act-fragments, until no one knows what anyone else is doing and
none understands how the fragments make a whole. Those in the
middle, performing necessary acts, are the most ignorant: shielded

from plan and outcome alike, they know neither what they do nor why. People on whom the consequences fall live in frustration. They have access to neither the design nor the execution of what affects them: they feel their fortunes ruled by unintelligible happenstance. The planners appear to be in charge, yet even they cannot control what happens at a distance from them. The reason is that social distance, the presence of facilitating agents between me and what I intend, denies me direct experience of the nature, circumstances, costs, and outcome of what is done. Without direct experience, plans cannot be adjusted to meet reality, preserve ideals, and fulfill even minimal moral requirements.

The lack of firsthand experience is of central importance here. Planners and leaders tend to have little idea of the way their designs are executed. Legislators, administrators, and bureaucrats make rules the application of which is in other hands and whose effects are unpredictable. There is not enough personal contact between decision makers and doers for there to be an understanding by either of the problems, circumstances, and point of view of the other. Executives tend to be so shielded from knowledge of the consequences of their ideas on individual persons that they can have little sympathy for those who suffer from their actualization. Outcomes are considered only in the aggregate and on statistical individuals; the effect of actions on the feeling subject, on the private soul, remains unobserved and hence uncalculated. As a result, those on the receiving end, and in one context or another that means all of us, find the entire process of making decisions and executing them unintelligible or unintelligent. Since it is easiest to explain untoward happenings as due to nastiness, we come to believe that the entire world is bent on frustrating our will. Institutions and those who occupy roles in them begin to be viewed with suspicion and social life acquires an undertone of fear and hatred.

This fragmentation of the social act occurs in proportion to its size and complexity. The more momentous and remarkable human achievements become, the more people are required for their accomplishment. These individuals operate in a tightly organized way, each making a contribution to the larger act, which no one could perform alone. Paradoxically yet naturally, increase in the integration of the social act brings with it a corresponding growth in fragmentation. The disconnectedness is evident when the situation is viewed from the standpoint of the individual; from the social perspective, for awhile at least, everything appears to be working effectively and well. The two perspectives are, of course, organically connected. It is precisely the increase in the size of our institutions that reduces the scope of individual contribution, and it is their complexity that submerges us in a sea of incomprehension. The broken world is, in this way, the psychological counterpart of the tightly ordered world of large-scale social acts. This, on first analysis, is the private cost of public good: the great wealth and stability of industrial society are created at the expense of the passivity and psychic impoverishment of its members. The pauperization is not to be measured by the standards of high culture. It is not the absence from our souls of refined taste and clever speculations, but of basic orientation about the world and our place in it. The loss of self-respect and self-understanding—the loss of self—it entails steals meaning and dignity from daily life.

MEDIATION

The breaking of the social act into its minute constituent parts begets a world of ignorance and irresponsibility. The dominant phenomenon behind the fragmentation is a social relation we can observe even in the most primitive societies. This is what I call "mediation," the cooperative action of humans on each others' behalf. Mediation occurs whenever someone or something is interposed between oneself and one's actions. The paradigm of such interposition is doing something for another specifically at his or her request. But mediation does not require conscious personal interaction. In its institutionalized forms, particularly in mass society, complex and indispensable social acts are performed on behalf of many without anyone having requested them. No one munching on Wendy's beef has ever asked an Iowa farmer to invest in steers, yet from farm to kitchen many thousands work to keep fries coming and hamburger buns filled.

In its most primitive form, mediation is simply the use of a tool to shield the body or to enhance effectiveness. The gloves I wear when I prune the rosebush are interposed between thorn and living flesh; they are the means used to protect my hands. Carpenters find it advantageous to drill the holes needed for bolts instead of trying to make them by scraping the wood with their nails. What makes these cases of mediation is the placement of a third between oneself and the object one works on or the result one attempts to achieve. The employment of instruments and means—the interposition of such mediating thirds—has served as the foundation of civilized life from its beginnings. Nevertheless, its essential rationality was not fully appreciated until Hegel's wholesale celebration of its virtues. Hegel saw mediation as all-pervasive: it was only the imposition of concepts, of negativity, of developmental stages that made the growth of consciousness—of organized human life—possible. Peirce, under Hegelian influence, declared mediation or Thirdness the category of rationality itself and announced that its increase is the ultimate evolutionary aim of Nature.

HEGEL AND PEIRCE ON MEDITATION

Hegel's vision of the ubiquity of mediation is not without basis. Cooperative labor involves the introduction of empowering others between one's project and achievement. Our institutions are sets of cooperative acts frozen into mediating structures. The language of communication consists of thirds—sounds and written marks or words and sentences—bridging the gap between minds. Inference, the work of thought, is itself a mediating process that attains conclusions by means of rules or interjacent premises. Yet Hegel went too far in denying all immediacy and, with it, the possibility of a private, subjective life. Peirce, fortunately, corrected Hegel's tragic denial: he saw that Firstness, the qualitative feel of things, is an irreducible and unsublatable element of reality. Thirds themselves, he remarked, have an aspect of firstness which is, roughly, the way laws and sign-cognitive sequences appear or feel in direct experience.

As a parenthetical remark, let me add that Hegel's rejection of immediacy entangled him in a thicket of mistakes. He failed, first of all, to do justice to consciousness as actually lived, to that flow of unreflective and unverbalized awareness of which much of everyday life consists. As a result, he left no room in his system for the privacy and individuality that escape description in universal terms, but which constitute the heartbeat of personal consciousness. And because of this misunderstanding of the nature of consciousness, he thought he could assign it to institutions, to states, and to an abstract, cosmic spirit seeking self-realization in history. Finally, misplacing consciousness led him to misplace the source of agency, as well: he thought that concepts, social forces, and such impersonal abstractions as reason are the ultimate causes of whatever takes place.

An adequate theory of mediation must rectify these errors. It must strike a proper balance between mediation and immediacy assuming, at the proper times, the perspective of individual awareness. It must restrict the assignment of consciousness to living animals. And it must lodge agency where it rightfully belongs, on the ontological level of particular persons. Without this, social life cannot be seen to have private costs at all. The truth is that "the litany of lamentations" of which, from the standpoint of suffering individuals, so much of history consists, constituted for Hegel neither loss nor cost. For he viewed the pain in its objectivity, the way scientists observe the death-struggle of flies caught in a spider's web or generals the discomfort of their starving soldiers. But suffering merely seen and described loses its hurt; it ceases to be pain. Without proper attention to the private soul, without deep sympathy for how things feel, theories of alienation remain laughable.

THE GROWTH OF MEDIATION

When the third I interpose between intention and accomplishment is an inert tool in need of manipulation by me, the cognitive distance between agent and consequence remains minimal. When all is said and done, *I* prune the rosebush and *I* drill the hole; my tools have no independent life. They work when I put them to work, and I know everything that is done, and how it gets accomplished, firsthand. There is, to be sure, a little cognitive slippage: the dentist learns the full nature of what he or she does only when the drill slips from the tooth and strikes his or her hand. But such ignorance of some dimensions of what we do is easily corrected and the co-presence of agent, act, and consequence tends, in the course of events, to provide ample remedy.

The matter stands differently when inert tools become distance-spanning and sophisticated or when our instruments acquire a life of their own. The bombardier, flying in a plane above the clouds, adjusts gauges and pushes buttons. Although his instruments will operate without him as little as a hammer, on its own, pounds nails, they are immensely sophisticated and the great distance they make possible between agent and ultimate effect denies him experience of what he brings about. He knows neither what his machines do nor how, and he is altogether unacquainted with the carnage that results. Such ignorance is sometimes disguised by job descriptions and general verbal accounts.

But language itself is a mediating tool that is weakest when used as a substitute for experience.

The psychic distance between agent and consequence is greatest when the instruments that fulfill our will are other human beings. Even a single person acting on our behalf can make it difficult for us to know what he or she accomplished and at the cost of what undesirable side-effects. The independent agency of others naturally takes them beyond our intentions and out of our sight. The reports we then receive of deeds performed for us at a distance always lack the richness and immediacy of witness. But here at least we are honored with reports; when mediation becomes large-scale and is institutionalized, no one discloses what is done for us. Of course, in many cases nothing is performed for any one of us uniquely. When I contract for electrical service, people do not set out to make me some power. The thousands of persons employed by the company simply generate electricity, and some of it can be for me if I agree to pay. So although it is not done uniquely for me, it is yet done for me, and there is no significant difference between asking a person to take my photograph and signing up with a company to turn on my lights. In both cases, another person or other persons act as the third required to carry out my intentions.

In large-scale mediated institutions, ignorance of what is done on our behalf becomes endemic. Actions are broken down into their most easily performed fragments and separate individuals are employed to perform each of them. The variety and intricate interconnectedness of these acts is so great as to escape the knowledge of most of us. We live, instead, in an impoverished psychic world in which the benefits of social labor are taken for granted. The paradigmatically individual case of driving a car presupposes mediated chains that beggar the imagination. In addition to design, finance, and marketing, approximately 18,000 parts must be manufactured and assembled. For this to be possible, steel, rubber, and plastic must first be made. Roads must be built with machinery and out of materials created by the coordinated effort of thousands. Finally, oil must be pumped, refined, and delivered to power the car. There is no driver who knows all that was done on his or her behalf or how these things were accomplished and at what human cost. We thus become grossly ignorant of our own actions and of the consequences, many deleterious, we help to cause.

WHOSE ACTION?

But, one might object, why suppose that actions performed on one's behalf are one's own? In simple cases it is not difficult to see that deeds done for me are, though mediated, mine. If I hire thugs to beat my neighbor's kids, law, morality and common sense agree that their act is at once also mine. It is obvious, therefore, that physical performance of an action is not necessary for the requisite relation of ownership to obtain. Such direct agency is not sufficient either, for I can engage in bodily activities under duress or in my sleep, which no reasonable person would attribute to *me*. Yet when the treatment plant dumps my untreated sewage in a pretty stream, the point becomes more difficult to appreciate. I did not dump the sewage, after all, and had I known of it, I would certainly not have had them do it on *my* behalf. It seems, therefore, that the act cannot be mine: not having done it, wanted it, or requested it surely leaves me innocent and unconnected to the harm.

In fact, however, there is no essential difference between hiring a thug or a physician and engaging the services of the sewage treatment plant. In each case, I contract to pay for activities I deem desirable or necessary, and through the agreement and through subsequent payments I acquire partnership in the enterprise. All such undertakings produce a mix of results ranging from the happy to the disastrous, both foreseen and unpredictable. The consequences come in a single bundle: we cannot pick and choose what we want to adopt as our own act and responsibility. I cannot argue that I only wanted to drive at 120 miles an hour, not to hit pedestrians.

To be sure, dealing person-to-person differs from agreement between a person and an institution in the size of the parties involved and the corresponding magnitude of ignorance on the side of the contracting individual. But whenever anyone else helps us with anything, there is a measure of ignorance about what exactly he or she does and how. That nescience, however pervasive it is and whatever portion of it resists correction, is not enough to render the other's action not mine as well, or to absolve me from responsibility.

The illusion of isolation and innocence is itself a creature of large-scale mediation. It derives from the psychic distance at which we find ourselves from acts and consequences in the creation of which we are partners. In institutions such partnership is established not by specific and conscious consent or physical participation in the questionable deed. Connection to the result through intermediaries is no less real than if I were to cause it single-handedly. I make the larger social act mine by offering even a small contribution to it as member of a mediated chain. Alternatively, I can appropriate it by my support, rendering payment for the benefits I gain. The navigator cannot convincingly use as an excuse that he did not drop the bombs, nor can I claim that I pay only for meat, not the death of animals.

My point is that in the mediated world small contributions to large acts make us partners in their costs and benefits. The acts are ours even if we do not precisely know their nature and cannot control their consequences. They are "bought" with money or through what we do to make them possible. If we gladly appropriate the good that comes of them, we cannot deny connection to the harm.

BENEFITS OF MEDIATION

Socially and morally, then, many acts are mine whose nature, or even existence, I do not know and which therefore I cannot appropriate. In our social actions, we belong to the tightly unified world. Mediated chains enable us to accomplish staggering feats: we extract oil from the depths of the sea and send humans into space. As the chains become ever larger and more closely integrated, we manage to achieve hitherto unthinkable control over nature. Human health has improved, life expectancy has grown, comfort has increased in the last hundred years far more than the boldest visionary would have dared to predict. The same advances are achievable wherever people organize themselves to act in mediated chains on each others' behalf. The gains are directly correlated to the size and complexity of the chains: greater social unities can perform more stunning social feats.

I spend time on this reminder of our remarkable achievements and pleasant lives partly because we tend to forget them and partly because I want to relate them to mediation as its desirable effects. Mediation provides social benefits so vast that without it life would yield us mainly misery. But such benefits come not without a cost: the dark side of our growing, integrated chains is the broken world of shriveled selves. The social benefits and their private costs belong together as joint results of mediation in such a way that an increase in one brings with it a corresponding expansion in the other.

Costs of Mediation

Manipulation

There are five major costs of large-scale mediation. The hungry or heedless manipulativeness we find all around us is the most evident. In mediated chains we deal with each other in terms of our roles. The roles are defined by tasks to be accomplished; effectiveness and efficiency serve as the structuring values of the chains. There is neither time, therefore, nor natural incentive to attend to our workmates as persons: their feelings, their hopes, their private histories are irrelevant to what needs to be done. We soon learn to view them as instruments, just as we are seen as tools by others in the chain. Everyone's aim is to elicit the desired response, to get what we want or need without regard for those who bear its cost.

The use of people as means to fulfilling our own desires is universally condemned by ethicists. But, too often, discussions of the immorality of manipulation restrict themselves to the individual level. Relatively few writers pay much attention to the social conditions which invite and help to institutionalize the use of humans through the greater part of their lives. Even fewer moralists see manipulation as a natural consequence of these arrangements and circumstances, rather than as the result of condemnable individual choices. I do not deny, in fact I strongly affirm, that even in institutions it is only individuals who do anything: they are the source and center of all agency. But the place to look when we attempt to understand the pervasiveness of manipulation is not greed, nastiness, or the perverted psychology of people, but the patterns of their interaction in large-scale institutions.

Mediation-analysis enables us to do just this. Rules govern our connection with one another in mediated chains and they require impersonal impartiality. The actions we perform become our jobs and our personal feelings must be left outside the office door. Our roles then swallow us and the people we deal with come to be seen as our employees, clients, or customers, that is, as occupants of roles themselves. While such an arrangement has the great value of efficiency and evenhandedness, its cost is the disappearance of the personal element from official relations, the reduction of living subjects to rigid, objective roles. Manipulation is a natural result; unconsciously we feel we can all engage in it with the best of conscience, for we use only services not people, and the purposes we promote are not narrowly personal and certainly not our own.

Passivity

Manipulation dehumanizes others; passivity destroys the person in- side each of us. By "passivity" I do not, of course, mean lack of assidu- ous labor. On the contrary, mediated chains keep us constantly engaged, busy with the minor tasks of a driven world. But we cannot feel active if the wellspring of action resides outside us, if we determine neither what we do, nor how, nor when. It is just this self-determination that medi- ated chains make impossible. When we fill institutional roles, we lack either the motive or the execution: I act not because *I* meant to, or I plan actions *I* will never perform. As a result, we are impelled but rarely motivated and, since contentment comes of achieving our aims, we feel pleasure but are not satisfied.

Such passivity can do more to darken an otherwise pleasant existence than any other single factor. Most of us labor the greater part of almost every day in circumstances over which we have little control. We deter- mine neither the aim nor the content of our work; we must instead be ready, in a machinelike way, to do what bosses or superiors command. The frustration of feeling that we are at the whim of others is exacer- bated by the tendency of mediated institutions to transmit communica- tion better down than up. The chains cannot function well without es- tablished lines of authority; directives from above must, therefore, be able to be conveyed rapidly and clearly. Inquiries and suggestions from below, by contrast, tend to be viewed as unproductive meddling. The result is not only that we feel buffeted by the winds of the great social world, but also that we find our cry unanswered. It is not that we who serve in the center of the chains always want things to go the way we imagine. But to retain membership in a community, we must have the sense that we are heard.

Impotence

The third major cost of mediation is our gnawing sense of powerless- ness, even impotence. We tend to view mediated chains as alien forces that compel and constrain us. The thought that we are powerless is an exaggerated but natural apprehension of reality: in mediated chains, the individual's power is minuscule. "The system" appears to have a life of its own and is insusceptible to personal control. What I do, who I vote for, how much I protest seem to make no difference; even as contributor to the social act, I am but temporary occupant of a position and can easily be replaced. Institutions are vastly more powerful than any individual and if they are seen as the self's antagonist, only paralysis and bitterness result. Even if I view them as my larger, better self, my impotence is not alleviated; as a cell in the body or a wave in the sea, I can only hope to hide or lose myself in them.

The received wisdom is that the way to deal with the powerlessness of individuals is to band together into action groups. Consumer organizations, citizens' lobbies, and grass-roots political committees are supposed to restore the might of the little man in much the same fashion as labor unions were to help us resist the economic muscle of large corporations. And in the formative stages of these associations, solitary agents can indeed make a difference and the lines of communication to the top tend to be open. But the extent of the individual's power is at once the measure of group impotence: only organizations of size can constitute a match for large institutions. The result is the inevitable growth of structures whose job it is to protect and enhance the influence of each of us, to the point where no one has much influence even in these structures.

Psychic Distance

Psychic distance takes at least two forms. The first is self-imposed to combat the effects of frustration and impotence. Since we feel we make no difference, we simply cease to care. We distance ourselves from the affairs of the world and learn to treat our role as but a job. We cease to identify with what we do and become functional schizophrenics in our social lives. In this way, we can protect the self from constant irritation and convert the pain of insignificance into cynical indifference.

The other form of psychic distance is unintentional: it is a natural result of mediation. Passivity comes of not framing the purposes for our actions: psychic distance is the outcome of not knowing their consequences. The persons who mediate my actions serve as a shield: their presence between me and what I help to cause denies me direct experience of my acts and what they produce.

There are some contexts in which a description of what occurs is as good as firsthand acquaintance. And for certain purposes, dealing in a cool verbal medium is actually better than the heat immediacy exudes. But when it comes to feeling and moral action, there is no substitute for direct experience; words are imperfect in expressing our joy and pain. Direct presence engages the emotions and sweeps all but the most rigid prejudices out of the way. There is a natural tie between our senses, our feelings, and our acts: the horror we see evokes both sympathy and the tendency to render aid. In distancing the consequences of our acts, mediation cuts off sensory presence and thereby the effective compassion it creates. Psychic distance, as the sensory ignorance of what we work, is at once the reason we lack a motive to improve our deeds, and thus find ourselves at peace with patent evil.

Irresponsibility

The two forms of psychic distance help lay the groundwork of widespread social and personal irresponsiblity. This last great cost of mediation surrounds us on all sides and reminds us that alienation is by no means only a matter of how we feel. A crushing sense of impotence about changing anything causes us to retreat into our jobs. Pervasive ignorance of how our jobs advance the social act makes it difficult to see that act as our own. Since we think we neither cause it nor can change it, we simply refuse to take responsibility for what goes on. The irresponsibility is not willful and it is not the outcome of a vicious nature. It is an understandable, innocent response grounded in our inability to embrace the social act as ours. The artlessness of our reaction, of course, does not make it morally right. We are thus faced with the frightful spectacle of well-meaning people supporting by their acts institutional cruelty of a scope they would, as private persons, never dream to cause.

INCREASING COSTS

As mediation increases, so do its costs. In addition to the increments in manipulation, passivity, impotence, psychic distance and irresponsibility attributable directly to growth in the size and pervasiveness of mediated chains, these costs also enhance each other. Being manipulated, for example, fosters passivity, and psychic distance reinforces our sense of impotence. All of them, in turn, make irresponsibility an attractive response, which again aids passivity and appears to make manipulation all right.

At first, it might seem that the benefits of mediation are social, while its costs are borne by private individuals. That is indeed the way many of us perceive the course of the modern world. Improvements in such public goods as sanitation and control over infectious disease appear to be accompanied by an increase in alienation, unhappiness, and the incidence of mental illness. Greater social wealth leads to ever more impoverished personalities. The integration of the social world seems to fragment our psychological unity and we feel as strangers even though we work together every day.

PRIVATE CONSCIOUSNESS

There is a good explanation of these phenomena ready at hand. Cooperative action builds ever greater social unities. Minds, by contrast, cannot be compounded. The growth of institutions is not matched, therefore, by the development of some larger, public consciousness. Private, individual awareness is the only sort there is and that consciousness undergoes, if anything, a curtailment of its scope as a result of mediation. So while the social world expands, the world of private reflection and understanding contracts relative to it. Consequently, the ordinary person comprehends less and less of the interconnections of social reality. And the less we know, the more we feel frustrated and shunted to the side. Innocent ignorance is the ground of much emotional disorder, and it is seeing just such disarray that makes us believe that the cost of public good is private pain.

THE PRIVATE AND THE PUBLIC

I think that there is a great deal of truth in this explanation. And yet the sharp contrast between public and private will not stand scrutiny. In the final analysis, it is simplistic to say that in the mediated world public benefits are bought with private grief. First, in the strictest sense, there are no *public* benefits. And, second, the disorder we face is far from solely private.

There are no public benefits because there is no such being as the public. To speak of it is to invoke an agreeable fiction, or to use shorthand to refer to a collection of individuals. To say that the collection is a community is not to add another entity to the individuals that constitute it but simply to indicate their relation to one another. The public consists of individuals and only the individuals are real. They alone enjoy a conscious direction to life and, therefore, they alone can be benefited or harmed. The point is obvious if we look at it with a clear, non-Hegelian eye. When an infectious disease is eliminated, it is not some faceless Leviathan, the public, that is free of it, but simply you and I. In this way, public benefits are the benefits of many private persons; the good that comes of mediation is no less yours and mine than are its noxious side effects.

The disorder in the world, moreover, is not merely psychological. The inner and the outer, feeling and behavior are not separate chambers without a door. Personal disorder shows itself in what we do, and what happens to our bodies shapes our minds. Passivity is a condition of our souls *and* of our behavior. Psychic distance is a mode in which we experience the world, but it quickly leads to irresponsible action. The fragmented world may have started in our hurting, private psyches, but it did not remain there for long. It has invaded the integrated world and now lives in its heart. Our great institutions are staffed by too few who care and many employees lack initiative. We are cynical of ideals that could move us and treat each other with suspicion or ill will. Public and private are like an old couple: in spite of disagreements, they are never far apart.

EXPLANATION WITHOUT SUPPOSED MALFUNCTION

I began with the human act shattered into its minute constitutents. Next I explained how this is brought about in a world where most of our acts are mediated. We then saw how mediation, particularly of the magnitude we find in populous industrial societies, comes with a full package of costs and benefits.

There are three great advantages of an account such as this. First, it makes sense of a wide diversity of facts by the application of a few simple, intelligible concepts. Unification in thought of the multiplicity of phenomena is what it means to understand, and this theory goes some distance in the direction of advancing that difficult task. Second, it does so, I note with satisfaction, without postulating any social malfunction or malformation. Most alienation theories begin by identifying some defective social condition and assign to it a special role in the generation of ill effects. As I have indicated, focus on such a single, pre-eminent cause, whether it be class struggle or the breakdown of class structure, private property or the desolation of the family, is always misleading. Not only is the world not so simple, this frame of mind also creates the illusion that by eliminating a single social problem, we can be on our way to utopia.

And how can we tell defective social structures from sound ones? This requires a standard of social health and that, in turn, substantial normative commitments. The third advantage of my theory is that it can give a description of the facts without some prior view of what is wrong or right. I am not averse to making moral judgments, but it is best to make them when the facts are in. Values too hastily embraced determine how we view the facts and subtly guide our choice of evidence. In this way, theories are shown true too easily, and yet our understanding of things is not improved.

EMPIRICAL TESTS OF THE THEORY

A theory of the sort I have proposed can be made more specific by displaying some of the theorems it generates. A number of these shed revealing light on our current condition.

1) Psychic distance increases proportionately with the increase in the number of mediators. This suggests that populous and highly integrated societies tend to have less immediacy, more ignorance of social function and more irresponsibility than relatively less developed ones. In corporations, it shows sheer size to be an impediment and thus a cost. There is, of course, the possibility of countervailing causes, but the *tendency* I describe should be detectable.

2) Control over the actions performed on one's behalf diminishes in proportion to the increase in the number of intermediaries. This suggests a serious problem for chains of command and bureaucracies, where central direction is viewed as essential and is difficult to attain. Rules of responsibility in the military must be framed in a way that takes this slippage seriously and serves to reduce it to a minimum. Obviously, the quality of communication in the chains is an additional variable affecting control. But the important consideration is that the sheer size of the mediated chain, independently of any special feature of it,

tends to reduce the extent to which central plans can be faithfully executed.

3) Decreased ability to see social acts as one's own (namely, "to appropriate" them) proportionately decreases the readiness to take responsibility for them. This theorem establishes a clear connection between psychic distance and one of its important social effects. The presence of the relationship is a vast and costly reality in socialist countries. But it operates also in large corporations, particularly ones in which employees have little say in the decisions and little understanding of the operations of the company.

4) The extent of the difficulty in approximating full agency in one's work is directly proportional to the effort to find alternative areas of full agency. By "full agency" I mean the unity in one person of aim, execution, and enjoyed achievement. Very few people can attain this in mediated chains. The result is a great growth in gardening, hobbies, and do-it-yourself crafts. Even the more passive types participate: they plan to raise a glass, down the beer, and then enjoy the effects. Our resistance to being told at home is itself a product of being told at work: we stand jealous guard over our self-determination in the evening because we act at others' bidding through the day.

Further theorems can be generated and refined without difficulty. One important feature of them is that they are testable. The theory readily begets a research program and, in addition to the sense it makes of widely diverse phenomena, it also holds out the hope of quantitative empirical confirmation.

DOES IT POINT TO ACTION?

Yet all of this may not be enough to please those whose interest in alienation theory is motivated primarily by the desire for social change. Such ameliorationists or revolutionaries are likely to view my ideas as pure theory, or perhaps a way of substituting understanding for action.

This view is, of course, unjust. It is true that an analysis in terms of mediation and psychic distance is unlikely to serve as the conceptual foundation of a revolution. But it *can* ground constructive social action to mitigate the costs of mediation. There are two important features of actions so based. They have as their source a confirmed and, I hope, correct theory, instead of themselves serving, in an odd way, as retroactive confirmations of the view. And because the theory makes no moral statement, actions can flow from it only by the way it engages the shared values of the community. If it enhances the self-knowledge of the society and if there is agreement that psychic distance, irresponsibility, and manipulativeness are costs, we can lay plans to reduce them. Such remediation, based in knowledge and free agreement, is the only worthy and feasible course in a democracy.

REDUCE MEDIATION?

What can we do to reduce the manipulativeness, passivity, ignorance, and irresponsibility that affect us as the result of widespread mediation? Since large-scale mediation entails major costs, it is natural to suggest that we reduce it. This seems an attractive course so long as we do not reflect on the organic way in which almost everything we think good is related. The connection between the astounding comforts we enjoy and the size and productive order of our society is not accidental. Those who wish to turn to some modest utopia in the name of the principle that small is beautiful must ask themselves how we could feed New York on the product of family plots. If the country were to consist of semi-autonomous small communities, what would become of travel and transportation, commerce and communication, disease control, education, and mass production without which we would find ourselves with ax and spinning wheel?

I am not saying, of course, that mediation could not be decreased a little here and there. There may well be too many mediators in the civil service and there ought not to be any between parents and child in love and moral education. But these are minor modifications in a structure which, because of its benefits, we cannot seriously think of abrogating. People in another day may have felt happy chewing half-rotten meat with wooden dentures; how many today would choose that over corn fed beef? Dealienation strategies must utilize realistic, not romantic, remedies. We must retain the immense benefits of large-scale industrial society—the health, the comfort, the broad scope of choice, the economic and psychological underpinnings of justice it provides—while we effectively mitigate its ill effects.

Is Education the Remedy?

If mediation yields too much for us to give it up, are we defenseless against its painful costs? Not entirely. But I must warn against the hope for easy fixes. Mediation is ubiquitous and it always causes unwelcome effects. Nowhere in life do we find final solutions; here also, we can look only for constant struggle to keep psychic distance low.

I have indicated before that at the heart of our problems is a discord between private psychological and public social reality. Integrated social acts are viewed by their individual participants as consisting of meaningless act-fragments. The magnitude of the act, when contrasted with the minuscule role single agents play in it, virtually assures its unintelligibility. Lack of direct acquaintance with the plans and outcome of institutional processes keeps ordinary people in ignorance of what is done, how it affects others, and in what ways their activities help in causing misery. The quiet frustration of this ignorance shows itself well in what thought and language do to pretend we understand institutions and their large-scale acts. We endow unwieldy organizations, such as IBM, with unity and causal power, and learn to view them as individual, even personal, agencies. In England people have not yet forgotten to refer to such social structures as "they," ever reminding themselves that institutions are but human beings suitably related. We have lost this wisdom and innocently speak of government and corporation as a single being denoted by an "it."

Since the problem is ignorance, the solution might appear to be education. Yet education, at least as it is practiced today, tends to increase psychic distance instead of reducing it. The reason is twofold. Mediated chains and the attendant division of labor, specialization, and fragmentation are as prominent in the acquisition and dissemination of knowledge as in other activities in our society. And much of education suffers from exclusive reliance on the mediation of words: in this way, direct experience is further impoverished, and thought and sensory exposure become unrelated realms. Education could help us only if it overcame its excessive reliance on the verbal and the conceptual, and devoted itself to the integration of theory and daily life, of schooling and society.

REGAINING IMMEDIACY

When it comes to reducing the costs of social life, remediation must mean reimmediation. The premier strategy for righting the imbalance between private psychological and public social reality and for reducing inhumanity and irresponsibility in mediated chains is to expose every part of the chain to every member of it. More generally, immediate acquaintance with the persons, actions and consequences mediation hides from us tends proportionately to decrease our psychic distance from them. Such immediacy, particularly when combined with explanations of the interconnectedness of the elements, naturally increases our understanding. But its special dealienating power comes from the way it engages the subjective powers and personal perspective of the individual. There is simply no match for the direct feel of reality conveyed by sensory encounter; nothing mobilizes the resources of the subject more effectively or shakes intellect, feelings, and will into action more quickly and in greater unison. To achieve such widespread immediacy in institutions and in society at large requires the formulation of explicit policies and considerable effort in putting them into effect. Openness in government and inside corporations makes it possible for all interested parties to learn what is being done and why. But passive openness is inadequate. Active steps must be devised to familiarize planners, doers, and those who enjoy or suffer the consequences with each others' situation and work. Chief executive officers cannot be strangers to the shipping room and janitors must have access to those in power. Immediacy and forthright communication allay suspicion, and if we understand what decisions are made and why, we find acceptance of them easier. Conversely, planners tend to be more realistic and more ready to adjust grand designs if they have firsthand knowledge of the problems of implementation and of unexpected side effects.

CURRENT EFFORTS AT REMEDIATION

We can see the beginnings of a dim recognition that exposing each part of a mediated chain to all the others is a good strategy for increasing both responsibility and productivity. Some management training programs require that young people rotate through all the major job types in the company. More and more chief executives talk over lunch with their workers or visit employees in distant factories. And quality circles break down the communications barriers between production line workers and managers, and thereby not only improve efficiency but also enhance the sense of all that they have a say and a stake in the company. Such activities, when they are sustained and not motivated by public relations posturing, are clearly dealienating in their effects. But we could improve upon them if dealienation initiatives were designed with a better understanding of what they are meant to remedy.

Immediacy within mediated chains improves our grasp of how complex social acts are constituted. When it is mated with helpful explanations, it also shows us the place and significance of our own contribution to such larger public actions. If it is extended to my co-workers in their private capacity, it will reduce manipulativeness by a significant measure. For colleagues outside the workplace reveal themselves as persons, as human beings with needs, fears, and obligations quite like mine. This personal dimension of our relation, even if not intimate, quickly overshadows narrow role-connected contact in the mediated chain. It is easy to manipulate others if we are strangers to their souls. It is much more difficult to use them without concern for their good or dignity, if we know their feelings, their hopes, their families.

IMMEDIACY AND EDUCATION IN POLITICAL LIFE

In societies such as ours, where bureaucratic regulation plays a rapidly increasing role, special attention must be paid to immediacy in public and political life. Until some years ago, the president of the United States used to set aside a few hours every week to greet and shake hands with whoever cared to visit. Although these must have been stiff and burdensome occasions, the tradition addressed a need that was real and pressing even when we had much less mediation. People who feel impotent and lost in the crowd find it of immense significance to be able to meet, to have access to, persons of real power. Political scientists and sociologists may think such desires naïve, but their dissatisfaction has a devastating effect on the body politic. For access is symbolic empowerment and most of us seek no more. *We* do not wish to be the ones to make the decisions; we want only the opportunity for direct communication, a serious hearing, and the frank disclosure of competing views.

A closer look at this communicative immediacy reveals that its essence is educational. The hearing afforded ordinary citizens is an opportunity for politicians and bureaucrats to learn. And an honest account of the considerations, pressures, and problems involved in the formulation and administration of policy is a better lesson in civics than any school can teach. Viewed in this light, the central task of government itself is educational: it must organize and orchestrate the reciprocal teaching and learning of the community. The ideal is to have as little power-enforced regulation as possible. But as an absolute minimum, government should forego coercive measures whenever vigorous persuasion or suitable incentives can accomplish the same effect. The vast spread of regulations expresses a loss of faith in the educability of the populace and a stupendous confidence that leaders need not or cannot learn anything from the dialogue that leads to persuasion.

ACCURATE INFORMATION, MUTUAL COMMUNICATION

It is extremely difficult to achieve person-to-person political immediacy in a country as populous as ours. We can go some distance with direct encounter; beyond that, we must rely on technological aids which provide a sort of secondary immediacy. Everyone can, at some point, spend some time with elected officials and with civil servants. The demand for immediacy is not so stringent that everyone must meet every representative and each new president: an experience or two, occasionally renewed, provides enough general insight. The informed imagination can then take over and render the problems and decisions of other office-holders vivid and easy to embrace.

But in order for the imagination to be informed, there must be a steady stream of accurate advice concerning public figures, problems, debates, and decisions. The media, especially television with its mediated immediacy, are well adapted to providing this. Seriousness of purpose is the high demand: if both media and politicians believe that their function is to educate adult human beings, sensational revelations, bombastic half-truths, and partisan lies will find less favor in their eyes. The other direction in the flow of information is no less important. Through invited complaints, call-ins, public hearings, small group meetings, and questionnaires, but not through impersonal opinion polls, public officials must continually seek instruction from their employers.

Such ongoing exchange makes each citizen a full member of the community and enables all to appropriate public decisions as their own.

STERN RULES OF RESPONSIBILITY

All of the measures I have discussed so far are benignly enlightening. There is also a sterner manner of enhancing immediacy. We are not very clear in our minds about the proper rules of responsibility in mediated chains. After the Second World War, for example, an American tribunal convicted General Yamashita and condemned him to death for atrocities, of which he was probably ignorant, committed by his troops. By contrast, the superior officers who probably knew of the My Lai massacre were not even prosecuted. On the one hand, our custom is to consider anonymity in the mediated chain tantamount to innocence. Yet, on the other, we sometimes pluck people out of the obscurity of the chains to punish or destroy them in the way of an example. Committee decisions usually mean immunity for the faceless functionaries who make them. Yet, from time to time, public anger cleans out the committees and removes even those members who strongly dissented from offending policies.

If we wish to increase moral concern in our society, we must render the consequences of our acts immediate. When the acts are institutional and our contribution to them is minuscule, we do not in the course of things come to see what we have wrought, and we have no special incentive to inquire. A revision of the rules for holding members of mediated chains responsible would provide the needed stimulus for them to learn what they help to cause. The change would have to make the rules consistent and more severe. Each contributor to a social act needs to be made answerable for its ill effects. The punishment should be proportional to the damage and to the person's contribution, but it must be substantial enough to make voluntary ignorance too costly. If people knew the harmful consequences their apparently innocent mediated actions produce, natural sympathy with the victims would tend to make them question their role in the chain. If they thought they would have to answer for noxious outcomes, self-interest would cause them not only to examine orders and procedures but also, when the evil is gratuitous or clear, to refuse participation.

A More Humane World

These suggestions for reducing the costs of mediation would, if implemented, make both the public world and our private lives significantly better. Those who now perform meaningless act-fragments would become acquainted with the others whose agency completes their act. Planners, doers, and those who deal with the consequences would each learn firsthand what the others contribute, what forces constrain their choice and how it feels to occupy their station. By exposing us to each other as persons, such immediacy fosters sympathy and expands the understanding. It gives each of us a sense of partnership in our joint undertakings. Only in this way can private consciousness apprehend the social act and adopt it as its own. When that happens, suspicion no longer pervades our relations: we are fellow humans equally needy and all caught.

Nothing I have said here is inconsistent with the desire of many and the tendency of some to decrease mediation in their private lives. Greater immediacy with Nature and expanded agency are possible for almost everyone. The first points to the enjoyment of sea, mountains, trees, animals, and the vegetable garden in the yard. The second means liberating competence with tools, with cars, with repairs around the house, and the special delight of immediacy with our acts when we perform them without hope of issue, as ends in themselves. Most important, we could all achieve greater immediacy with each other in dialogue and shared activities. Telephone and television are mediating marvels of genuine usefulness. But we need not allow them to deprive us of the ultimate value of our eyes meeting and of hands that touch.[1]

NOTES

1. I wish to express my thanks to Professors John Howie and Henny Wenkart for helpful suggestions in formulating these ideas.

5

The Gift of Life: Ethical Problems and Policies in Obtaining and Distributing Organs for Transplantation
James F. Childress

PROBLEMS, POLICIES, AND PRINCIPLES

Society has entered a new era of organ transplantation. Solid organ transplantation began with the first kidney transplant in 1954, and in 1980 there were 4,697 kidney, 36 heart, and 15 liver transplants in the United States.[1] In the 1980s the number of transplants has increased dramatically, largely because of developments in immunosuppressive therapies, particularly cyclosporine. In 1984 there were 6,968 kidney, 373 heart, and 308 liver transplants. In 1985 the number of heart and liver transplants almost doubled again, while kidney transplants increased by more than 800.[2]

Despite such dramatic increases in transplants, the new era of transplantation has been marked by a persistent shortage of organs, a problem that has led to vigorous debates about policies to increase the supply of organs and to distribute them fairly. In addition to several state task forces, the National Organ Transplant Act (Public Law [PL] 98–507), which was signed into law on October 19, 1984, established a Task Force on Organ Transplantation to conduct by early 1986 a comprehensive review of medical, legal, ethical, social, and economic issues in transplantation.[3] An Office of Organ Transplantation was established within the Public Health Service of the Department of Health and Human Services. And there has been vigorous debate in bioethics about appropriate policies of procurement and distribution. (In this discussion attention will be focused on solid or viable organs rather than tissues because the former are often life-prolonging, are more expensive, and raise more difficult questions such as the determination of death.)

Although enough cadaver organs exist, society has not yet found an effective, efficient, and morally acceptable way to obtain them. The Council of Scientific Affairs of the American Medical Association has noted:

> Organs removed from a cadaver after breathing and heart action have ceased have sustained serious ischemic injury and, except for cornea, bone, and skin, are rarely suitable for transplantation. Death from brain injury, tumor, or infarction may permit hours or days of normal circulation, especially if controlled mechanical ventilation is maintained, which will allow preservation of heart and kidney until they can be removed, cooled, and properly preserved for transplantation. *There are more than enough deaths in the United States (estimate, 20,000) [of approximately two million deaths each year] to provide a surfeit of organs, if there were a satisfactory method of bringing all such cadavers into the pool of donors.*[4]

Yet in 1984 only 5,264 cadaver kidneys were transplanted in the United States. The remainder of the 6,968 kidneys that were transplanted came from living donors. Since each cadaver usually provides two kidneys and since approximately 20 to 25 percent of the donated kidneys are not used for various reasons (e.g., no matched recipient is available), it is reasonable to suppose that there were approximately 3,300 donations of cadaver kidneys—far short of the number needed for the estimated eight to ten thousand dialysis patients who are waiting for renal transplants. Thus, in this era of transplantation, patients face major shortages of organs.

Currently in all fifty states and the District of Columbia the Uniform Anatomical Gift Act (UAGA),[5] which was rapidly enacted in the late 1960s and early 1970s, allows us to determine what will be done with our organs after our deaths. The main mechanism is the organ donor card, available in many states with driver's license. Even if we do not sign a donor card, our families may donate our organs after our deaths, unless we have clearly objected to such a donation. Since the late 1960s opinion polls have indicated that large numbers of Americans are willing to donate their organs or their relatives' organs after their deaths. According to a 1985 Gallup Poll (conducted in late 1984),[6] among the people who were aware of organ transplants (93 percent), 85 percent indicated that they were very or somewhat likely to donate organs of their deceased loved ones, while 45 percent were very or somewhat likely to donate their own organs. The last percentage has declined dramatically since the late sixties, when, according to some polls, 70 percent of the adult population were willing to have their organs used for transplantation after their deaths,[7] but, in general, public support for organ donation remains strong. This reported, hypothetical support does not however, translate into actual donations. Few people (between 1.5 percent and 19 percent, according to some studies)[8] actually sign their donor cards for reasons that I will discuss later. Furthermore, families frequently find it very difficult to donate a deceased loved one's organs, and physicians and other health care professionals are understandably reluctant to raise the question of organ donation with grieving families.

Even though the UAGA allows the next of kin to donate a decedent's organs after his or her death, unless the decedent previously objected, its basic philosophical orientation appears in its recognition of the individual's right to determine the use of his or her organs, regardless of the family's wishes. The focus is the individual's premortem decision, symbolized by the donor card, and, in principle, the individual's will is determinative. This orientation marks the UAGA's fundamental departure from some major doctrines in the Anglo-American common law tradition. For many centuries the church was in charge of dead bodies under English law, which did not recognize any living person's property rights in a corpse and thus refused to maintain civil action against someone who had appropriated or mutilated a corpse (though it was possible to sue for damage to the monument). Early American legal decisions reflected the "no property" rule and American law regulated disposal of bodies only to the extent required for decency and public health, but by the early twentieth century several American courts had recognized the next of kin's "quasi-property" rights in the corpse.[9] Property rights may include the rights to control, use, exclude others from use, and transmit for various reasons, including commercial purposes. The next of kin's quasi-property right in a corpse did not include the right to use or transfer the corpse or its parts for commercial purposes; it was mainly a right to bury the body, correlated with an obligation to do so. The next of kin also had a derivative right to receive the body in the condition it was at the time of death. Several courts held that a decedent's will could not dictate postmortem disposition of the body on the grounds that the body is not property and thus not part of the decedent's estate. Later some courts began to recognize the individual's own quasi-property right in his or her body, at least to the extent of determining the place and mode of disposal, as well as permitting an autopsy. But such decisions did not clearly and directly recognize the individual's right to donate his or her body or its parts for use in science or medicine. In one famous case[10] in 1964, the will of Grace Metalious, the author of *Peyton Place*, directed that "no funeral services be held" and that her body be given to a medical school for research. The family objected, and the court upheld their objection, even though its reasons suggested circumstances when the decedent's will could triumph over the next of kin's wishes. As organ transplantation spread, statutory law was similarly chaotic.

This legal history sets the context for the UAGA, which recognized both the decedent's and the next of kin's limited quasi-property rights in the corpse but assigned priority to the decedent's express wishes. In the late sixties, several analysts of the UAGA worried about its impact on the family's quasi-property rights in the corpse. However, practice has not followed the law. Hospitals and procurement agencies do not "excise an organ without the express permission of the decedent's family —regardless of the existence of a donor card,"[11] even though, according to the UAGA, the family has no right to override the decedent's express wish to donate (or not to donate). Hospitals and procurement agencies depend on public goodwill and want to avoid conflicts with the family, adverse publicity, and legal actions even though the UAGA exempts their good faith conduct from civil and criminal liability. In practice in the United States, the individual's will to donate does not prevail; it is subject to family veto.

The language of organ transfer reflects the concepts and norms of "gift" and "donation." The only officially recognized mode of transfer is characterized as a gift or donation. (Although the UAGA authorized individuals or the next of kin to give or donate organs, it did not explicitly rule out the sale of organs, which I will discuss later.) The motifs of gift and donation dominate not only the legal framework but also the most important literature on the transfer of organs and tissue.[12] Yet, some ambiguities remain because of the two potential donors of organs, the individual and the next of kin, as well as the use of the term "donor"

to refer to (1) the decision-maker about donation or to (2) the actual
source of the organs, whoever made the decision. Other ambiguities result from the complex moral realities that huddle under the umbrella of
"gift" and "donation." Gifts are not always free and spontaneous; they
may be obligatory, as in various gift exchanges. And they are not always
disinterested or altruistic because they are often motivated by the individual's interest in himself or herself or in some people other than the
recipient of the gift. Unfortunately, many analysts of organ transplantation appear to assume that a gift must be nonobligatory and purely altruistic, overlooking the complex mixture of norms and motives in most
gifts, including organs.[13] Nevertheless, the system of organ procurement
in the United States is best characterized as "encouraged altruism."

Although gifts are more complex than is often recognized, their connection with major moral and religious beliefs is significant. Against
some tendencies in contemporary culture, the Jewish and Christian traditions emphasize the embodied self rather than a sharp dualism between spirit and body.[14] This emphasis supports a principle of respect
for persons that is not limited to their (disembodied) spirits but also includes their bodies, both before and after death. Stewardship over nature
can include an agent's stewardship over his or her own body and over
corpses that are entrusted to him or her, but this dominion of stewardship is limited. Although Jewish law prohibits deriving benefit from,
mutilating, or delaying the burial of a corpse, this prohibition can be
overridden to save a life. There is a debate about how immediate and
certain the rescue must be, but, in general, Judaism recognizes the right
to donate bodily parts, emphasizing that the death of the donor must be
definitely established. Roman Catholics and Protestants alike tend to
support organ donation, believing that God's power to resurrect the
body will not be thwarted by prior dispersal of its parts. (However,
some Christians do appeal to their belief in bodily resurrection as one
reason for their unwillingness to donate organs [12 percent in the 1985
Gallup poll], and some respondents indicated that organ donation was
against their religion [9 percent]).[15] All of these traditions have rituals
and symbols of respect for the dead that, for the most part, are not inconsistent with the donation of organs and tissue, either by the individual or
by others on his or her behalf. However, these traditions have generally
not interpreted their religious-moral norms to obligate postmortem organ
donation even though they tend to permit and even to praise it. Even
though policies to increase the supply of organs may anticipate the as-

sistance or at least the acquiescence of most religious groups, they cannot ignore opposition to organ donation among such groups as Christian Scientists and some Protestant sects.

In this legal, social, and cultural context, potential donors often respond enthusiastically to dramatic cases involving identified lives, as in the case of Jamie Fiske, but changes in public policies may be necessary in order to increase the supply of organs for unidentified strangers. Ad hoc appeals by the president, the secretary of Health and Human Services (HHS), or some other notable, on behalf of some needy person, usually a child, have sometimes been effective, but there is debate about the fairness of singling out one individual when so many are in need. One justification offered for such special appeals is that they increase the overall donation of organs and thus redound to the benefit of many others. However, such appeals cannot be expected to work over time, and people in need often resent the attention some individuals receive because of their financial resources or special connections. Thus, there are good reasons to seek more systematic approaches.

Some changes in public policies would probably increase the supply of organs and tissues and thus produce the greatest good for the greatest number (utility) without violating other important ethical principles and values such as respect for persons, including their autonomous wishes and their bodies, and justice in the distribution of burdens and benefits. Other values have also been emphasized—the involvement of the family and the promotion of community through acts of sharing and generosity. These principles and values are embedded in our practices and institutions, including our religious traditions, and they are supported by several ethical theories.[16] However, there is disagreement about how they should be applied (e.g., how much weight should be given to the family's wishes in relation to the decedent's prior wishes.)

It is important to distinguish ethical acceptability, ethical preferability, and political feasibility. Within the range of ethically acceptable policies, some may be ethically preferable or ideal without being mandatory, and some may be politically feasible, while others are not. In view of these distinctions, the major questions are: (1) Which policies would probably reduce scarcity and thus save lives and/or improve their quality—a morally desirable goal—without transgressing moral limits, and, of these morally acceptable policies, which are morally preferable and which are politically feasible? (2) Which policies of allocation and distribution of scarce organs are ethically acceptable, ethically preferable, and politically feasible? Judgments about ethical acceptability and preferability invoke the whole range of moral principles and values identified earlier.

POLICIES TO INCREASE THE SUPPLY OF ORGANS

Educational Efforts

Most public educational efforts have focused on individuals as the donors of their own organs through signed donor cards. In the late 1960s there was reason to think that such efforts might be effective within the UAGA. However, in view of the actual practices of donation and procurement that have evolved, those efforts need to be supplemented by attention to individuals as familial decision-makers. Not only are donor cards not determinative in practice (though most families also give their consent when the decedent has signed a donor card), but, more significantly, few cards are actually signed, cards are often not found after an accident, and cards rarely result in actual organ donations.

There are several reasons for people's reluctance to sign donor cards. In the 1985 Gallup poll, two reasons were most frequently given as "very important": "they might do something to me before I am really dead" (23 percent) and "I'm afraid the doctors might hasten my death if they needed my organs" (21 percent). These two reasons reflect distrust in health care professionals in this context, and this distrust is probably not amenable to public education (though clarification of brain death would help to allay some fears). The next two most common reasons for reluctance to sign donor cards were a dislike of "thinking about dying," and a dislike of "the idea of somebody cutting me up after I die." When these points are combined with two other points from the 1985 Gallup poll, there is a very strong case for concentrating on individuals as familial decision-makers rather than on individuals as signers of donor cards. First, 85 percent indicated that they were very or somewhat likely to donate the organs of a relative, and 65 percent were very or somewhat likely to donate the organs of their children. Second, 63 percent approved of the following statement: "Even if I have never given anyone permission, I wouldn't mind if my organs were donated upon my death." [17] These figures are in sharp contrast to the 45 percent who said that they were very or somewhat likely to donate their own organs. The willingness to donate organs is even lower among blacks and other groups who perceive themselves to be on the margins of society and who tend to distrust the society.[18]

Many factors probably contributed to the decline in the public's trust in health care professionals as reflected in the tremendous increase in medical malpractice suits in the 1970s. For example, the historical linkage between organ transplantation and efforts to update the concept and criteria of death by recognizing brain death may have contributed to the widespread suspicion that there is risk of being declared dead prematurely to benefit others if one is on record as an organ donor.[19] In general, the factors that contributed to the decline in trust appear to have had more impact on individuals' decisions about donor cards than on families' decisions about a relative's organs. Many individuals fear that signed donor cards will put them at the mercy of professionals who may sacrifice them to benefit others. Putting control in the hands of families alleviates some of these fears.

Required Request/Routine Inquiry

"Required request," "routine notification," or "routine inquiry"— proposed by Arthur Caplan[20]—is the policy option that is currently gaining momentum and appears to be justified in view of the moral values and political realities surrounding organ donation. There are at least two versions of this approach: the target might be either the potential individual donor or the next of kin, and the time of the request, notification, or inquiry would differ accordingly.

On the one hand, the individual might be asked to make a decision about whether to donate his or her organs, perhaps in conjunction with obtaining a driver's license. For the reasons indicated above, there are doubts that such an approach would significantly increase the number of organ donors (though signed donor cards facilitate discussions with the decendent's next of kin). Indeed, in view of the reasons people give for their reluctance to make an advance decision and record it on donor cards, it is possible that many people would say no and then their negative advance decision would preclude familial donation after their deaths.

On the other hand, a policy could require hospitals to ask surviving family members whether they would like to donate a decedent's organs. This version is more promising because of its focus on the next of kin. It recognizes that families may gladly make a gift of life if asked even though they may not actually initiate such a donation. Generosity in response to an inquiry or request is still active, rather than passive, and policies should express and support such generosity. According to some pilot studies in hospitals, such a policy of routine inquiry is feasible and it could increase the supply of organs without sacrificing important moral values.[21]

These different formulations—required request, routine notification, and routine inquiry—are not mere matters of semantics, particularly since the idea of requirement is anathema to many. However, the goal is routine notification or inquiry, and the question is whether society through legislation or processes of accreditation should require institutions to establish mechanisms to ensure routine notification or inquiry. The language of notification or inquiry emphasizes the right of families to know about the possibility of organ donation under appropriate circumstances. For many the term "request" is too strong, and they argue that the actual approach should be to offer family members an opportunity for a donation, which may enable them to find meaning in tragic circumstances. Many have also argued that inquiries should not be mandated in all circumstances (e.g., where the death has occurred under circumstances that preclude the retrieval of transplantable organs) and that conscientious objection should be allowed (e.g., a family may request "no request").

It is not surprising that several hospitals have already instituted policies of routine inquiry, several states have either adopted, or are currently considering, legislation to require hospitals to establish such policies, and that the Task Force on Organ Transplantation endorsed routine inquiry.[22] A policy of routine inquiry is ethically acceptable: it would help to meet the need for organs without violating other moral principles. It is ethically preferable to a policy of presumed consent because it expresses and supports active generosity, even though family members respond to an inquiry or request for a gift rather than offering it on their own initiative. It is also politically feasible because it focuses on the family rather than the individual, hospitals rather than professionals, and explicit rather than presumed consent. It too presupposes educational efforts, particularly efforts directed at clarifying brain death.

Even though the policy of required request or routine inquiry would focus on familial decision-makers rather than on individual donors, there are good reasons to correct the practical asymmetry between individuals' advance decisions for and against donation. According to the UAGA, both decisions are equally binding. The individual's express wish not to donate, if known, is honored by organ procurement teams.

But in practice organs are rarely if ever removed without the family's permission even when there is a valid donor card. At the very least it would be useful to educate professionals about their exemption from civil and criminal liability when they act in good faith on a donor's wishes, regardless of the family's wishes. In addition, it may be appropriate to consider legal sanctions to ensure that individuals' wishes to donate are not violated.

Presumed Consent

Both the UAGA and required request involve "contracting in" or "opting in," and there are good ethical arguments for giving them priority over a policy of "contracting out" or "opting out." These arguments include the support for and expression of a community of active generosity (whether it takes the form of initiating a donation or responding to a request for a donation). However, a policy of presumed consent (sometimes called the "routine salvaging of organs" or "harvesting organs") may not be ethically unacceptable, even if it is ranked lower than some other policies. It has already been implemented for corneas in a dozen states in the United States, and it exists for organs in several countries, including Denmark, France, Israel, Norway, Spain, Sweden, and Switzerland. In approximately half of the countries with presumed consent statutes, physicians are also required to determine whether the family objects to organ removal, and some countries recognize donor cards along with presumed consent. Although countries with presumed consent legislation still have waiting lists for renal transplantation, they "seem to come closer to meeting their needs for transplant kidneys." [23]

A policy of presumed consent does not presuppose that bodily parts are property "owned" by the society, which may claim them upon a person's death. Rather it shifts the presumption about a person's wishes apart from his or her explicit and active statements about those wishes, and, with this presumption, physicians and other professionals would probably find it easier to approach families about permission to remove a dead or dying relative's organs. In short, it could provide the basis for a ritual in a difficult, often tragic, "boundary situation." [24] Recognition of presumed consent as the basis for organ removal—or at least as the basis for a request to the next of kin—does not necessarily violate principles of justice and respect for persons, if the decedent has a real opportunity to dissent. Also, it would not exclude active generosity, for individuals could still donate their own organs; it would only presume generosity where individuals have not explicitly dissented.

Even though the language of presumed consent is very common, the policy under consideration might better be viewed as one of tacit consent. Presumed consent sometimes encompasses, but is sometimes distinguished from, tacit consent and implied consent. Among the several varieties of consent, the paradigm case of consent that creates rights in others is express or explicit consent. Although tacit consent is distinguished from explicit consent, it is not unexpressed. It is rather expressed passively or silently by omissions and by failures to indicate or signify dissent (e.g., when a person does not object verbally or in other ways to a proposed kiss).

As John Simmons notes, the failure to dissent or object constitutes tacit consent only under certain conditions: the potential consenter must be aware of what is going on and that consent or refusal is appropriate, must have a reasonable period of time for objection, and must understand that expressions of dissent will not be allowed after the period ends; he or she must understand the accepted means for expressing dissent; these means must be reasonable and relatively easy to perform; and, finally, the effects of dissent cannot be "extremely detrimental to the potential consenter." [25] Some of these conditions ensure the consenter's understanding; others ensure the consent's voluntariness. When these conditions are met, the potential consenter's silence may be construed as tacit consent. Consent is signified, but passively. One major difficulty is determining whether silence indicates a lack of understanding rather than tacit consent. In contrast to tacit consent, implied consent, or implicit consent, is not expressed or signified; it is rather inferred from other actions. For example, a patient's consent to one life-saving procedure may imply consent to another life-saving procedure. Although a person may engage in actions that imply consent, or from which others may infer consent, he or she may not have understood such an implication. Thus, in contrast to tacit consent, implied consent does not presuppose an intention to consent.

If consent is presumed on the basis of a person's failure to dissent under certain conditions, it is tacit consent; if it is presumed on the basis of a person's other actions, it is implied or implicit consent. If, however, it is presumed on the basis of a general theory of human values without any reference to this person's action, it is very different (e.g., an accident victim's presumed consent to an emergency procedure), and it may be morally suspect when the action to which a person's consent is presumed primarily benefits others (e.g., organ donation or nontherapeutic experimentation). Most often the consent that is presupposed by presumed consent policies of organ procurement is tacit consent, rather than the other versions of presumed consent. However, because silence may indicate a lack of understanding of the means of consent and dissent or of the proposed course of action, a policy of organ procurement based on tacit consent is not morally acceptable without vigorous efforts to ensure public understanding. In view of the moral necessity of such educational activities, presumed consent legislation may not be more cost effective than increasing, improving, and redirecting educational activities within the context of the UAGA.

A policy of presumed consent does not appear to be politically feasible now. Although it might have been possible in the late 1960s to institute a policy of presumed consent—for example, Paul Ramsey[26] thought that it was a close moral call between UAGA and presumed consent—it would now be difficult, probably impossible, to modify the policy of "contracting in" of the UAGA, especially because of the decline of trust in physicians and other health care professionals. When the 1985 Gallup poll asked, "Do you feel that doctors should have the power to remove organs from people who have died recently but have not signed an organ donor card without consulting next of kin," 86.5 percent said "no."

The role of the next of kin varies in different presumed consent laws: some require that the next of kin be consulted to see if they dissent, while others make the presumed consent of the deceased determinative. However, the actual practices are much the same whatever the legal framework.[27] For example, even in France, where the policy of presumed consent does not require familial approval or ratification, physicians and other professionals still seek familial consent.[28] In view of the social values identified earlier, it is unlikely that presumed consent legislation would, in principle or in practice, ignore familial wishes not to donate. But then it would arguably be better simply to require that the family be approached—the routine inquiry policy—rather than for the state or professionals to presume the patient's consent. However, there are at least two ways to understand the family's authority to donate organs. On the one hand, that authority itself may be viewed as resting on the decedent's presumed consent, now presumed by the family rather than by the state or professionals. On the other hand, that authority may be viewed as resting on the family's quasi-property right in the corpse, as long as the decedent did not clearly express his or her wishes.

MONEY, TAX CREDITS, AND FAMILY CREDITS FOR ORGANS

The Sale of Organs

It would be possible to obtain organs for transplantation by purchasing them for delivery from a living vendor (e.g., a kidney from a person who has two healthy kidneys or renewable tissue such as bone marrow) or from cadavers. Contrary to a common supposition, the UAGA does not prohibit a market in organs. Nevertheless, because of proposals to establish organizations to broker human kidneys by arranging worldwide sales, some states (e.g., California, Maryland, Michigan, New York, and Virginia) have passed laws to prohibit a market in organs, and the National Organ Transplant Act of 1984 (PL 98–507) prohibited the transfer of "any human organ for valuable consideration if the transfer affects interstate commerce." [29] Earlier there was a market in blood, and Robert Steinbrook contends that "in the US, sentiment against tissue sales is reflected in the fact that an all-volunteer blood supply was established." [30] In fact, the shift away from a market in blood—though blood plasma and some products are still sold—resulted not from widespread moral revulsion, but from the cogent arguments, offered by Richard Titmuss, among others, that the commercial system in blood was ineffective, inefficient, and dangerous.[31]

Even if the voluntary, noncommercial system is ethically preferable, because it expresses and supports generosity, there is still debate about whether the sale of organs and tissue is ethically unacceptable apart from questions about its effectiveness, efficiency, and safety. For example, Pope Pius XII held that the question of compensation for cadaver organs, especially corneas, was unresolved.

> Moreover, must one, as is often done, refuse on principle all compensation? This question remains unanswered. It cannot be doubted that grave abuses could occur if payment is demanded. But it would be going too far to declare immoral every acceptance or demand of payment. The case is similar to blood transfusions. It is commendable for the donor to refuse recompense: it is not necessarily a fault to accept it.[32]

As George Mavrodes suggests,[33] we can put the sale of organs in two contexts: the sale of various goods and the transfer of organs. In the first context, the question is what is morally problematic about the sale of human organs among the various goods traded in the marketplace; in the second context, the question is what is morally problematic about the sale of human organs among the various ways to transfer such organs. If the response is that we do not "own" our bodies, or the bodies of deceased relatives, and thus cannot sell their parts, the respondent then has to indicate how people can "give" or "donate" what they do not own. Of course, one answer is that people can have quasi-property rights in the body and its parts, but this answer begs the question unless it also indicates why property rights in the body and its parts should be limited in this way.

Among the reasons offered for permitting if not encouraging a market in organs and tissue, two are most prominent: (1) a market could alleviate the shortage of organs and tissue for transplantation in order to save and improve lives, and (2) a market would respect the freedom of individuals to do what they want to do with their lives as long as they do not harm others.[34] The main rejoinder to the first argument is that there are other effective, safer, and ethically preferable ways to increase the supply of organs. The main rejoinder to the second argument is that individuals are not acting freely but are being exploited when they dispose of their bodily parts in a commercial transaction. Opponents tend to focus on several problems in a market in organs: the risks of sales to recipients (e.g., poorer quality of organs); the risks of sales to vendors (e.g., the risks of removal of a kidney from a living vendor) or to potential sources of organs (e.g., they might be killed or allowed to die prematurely so that others could sell their organs); and the vendor's lack of voluntariness, especially if he or she is poor, economically vulnerable, and subject to exploitation.[35] Opponents also contend that a commercial system would be costly and would drive out altruism.

Nevertheless, even if the negative consequences for the vendor, the recipient, and the system of giving and receiving could be avoided and the vendor's voluntariness could be attested, opponents would still insist that a commercial market in organs is abhorrent to our system of values because it is similar to prostitution or even to slavery in treating human bodies as property and commodities.[36] They ask what kind of society is symbolized and reflected in various policies toward the transfer of bodily organs. The critical question for them is whether society's policies toward organ transfer both express and sustain a community in which human bodies are treated justly and respectfully. These critics contend that such a community and its values would be threatened by a market in organs.

Most of the arguments for and against a market in organs have been presented in general terms without an indication of whether they apply to both living vendors and cadavers, whose use might be controlled by the person while alive or by the next of kin after his or her death. Perhaps the most vigorous opposition to a market centers on living vendors, but some major fears of abuse center on cadavers (e.g., people might be killed to obtain their organs). Nevertheless, arguments about dehumanization and about abuse need to be more specific because it is not clear that they apply equally to all types of organs and tissues. For example, for living sources, it may be important to distinguish renewable from nonrenewable tissues.[37]

Tax Credits

Serious proposals have emerged, for example, from Congressman Philip Crane, to amend the Internal Revenue Code to provide income and estate tax deductions for decedents who donate organs for use in transplantation.[38] One such proposal would allow a deduction for the decedent's last taxable year of $25,000 for each qualified transplant donation. For many, such indirect incentives may be more acceptable than direct payments. However, it is important to consider not only their effectiveness, efficiency, and consequences, but also how they really differ, if at all, from direct payments. It may be instructive to ask how the line is drawn between direct payment and coverage of a donor's medical expenses, compensation of a living donor's lost wages, and payment for the burial expenses of a deceased donor. If the line can be drawn in a satisfactory way, some objections to a policy of tax credits might decline. However, such a policy would benefit the middle and upper classes, not the poor, and might be objectionable on this ground.

The Family Credit Policy—Priority for Donors of Organs

Some ethicists—for example, Paul Ramsey and William May—have held that a system of family credits for organ donations might be ethically acceptable in the transfer of organs and, in any event, is preferable to the public sale of organs. Ramsey holds that "families that shared in the premortem giving of organs could share in freely receiving if one of them needs transplant therapy," and May would credit the family with "appropriate units against the day that one of its members may require an organ." [39] Such a policy may appear to be attractive at first, in part because of its connection with family values, which are so important in organ donation. It can also avoid treating organs as mere commodities and crass commercialization, which threatens a market in organs. But the putative advantages of such a policy may be deceptive, and the policy may even jeopardize the voluntary, cooperative system of organ donation to benefit unidentified strangers in the community.

Defenders of this policy point to the United States system of blood donation which allows participants to acquire family credits. However, the blood donor and his or her family do not acquire priority to receive blood when it is in short supply; they are only exempted from having to pay for or to replace the blood they use. Similarly, many would argue, it is not justifiable for families of organ donors to have priority over other persons in need of organs. To allow such priority would subvert the current voluntary, cooperative, altruistic system. The willingness to contribute organs to the system of procurement and distribution depends in part on the perception that the organs will be distributed fairly according to acceptable public criteria, that they will not be wasted, and so forth. A policy of family credits would emphasize particularistic motives (i.e., the desire to benefit one's own family in case of need) over universalistic motives (i.e., the desire to benefit others in need), and in the long run it might threaten the voluntary, cooperative system as much as the sale of organs.

LIVING DONORS

For kidneys and segmental pancreatic transplants and for some renewable tissue, such as bone marrow and blood, it is possible to use living persons as sources. Some recent controversial cases have involved bone marrow transplantation. In one case, the Supreme Court of Iowa refused to order a hospital to disclose the name of a potential bone marrow donor to a twenty-seven-year-old man who was dying of leukemia and might have been helped by bone marrow transplantation.[40] The leukemia patient had learned from a technician at the hospital that an apparently suitable donor was listed in the computer files. In another case,[41] a judge refused to order a man to complete the tests he had started and to donate bone marrow to save his cousin's life if he proved to be histocompatible. The principle of autonomy or respect for persons and derivative rules, such as privacy, dictate a policy of not removing tissues or organs from a person's body against that person's will even to save someone else's life. This principle is recognized in both morality and law. It is sometimes interpreted to permit removal of organs from an incompetent person, such as a minor or retarded person, who cannot give valid consent, but often the explicit rationale in those cases is that the "donor" will also benefit (e.g., by not losing a close sibling). In such cases, proxy consent is required.

Living donors now provide a smaller proportion of the kidneys for transplantation than earlier. In 1967, 56 percent of the transplanted kidneys came from cadavers, while in 1973, 70.4 percent came from cadavers, and in 1982, 68.7 percent came from cadavers.[42] Yet in contrast to many other countries, the United States still obtains approximately 25–30 percent of its transplanted kidneys from living donors. Listed below are the figures for 1980–84,[43] which indicate a decline from 1983 to 1984 in the number as well as the proportion of kidneys obtained from living donors:

Year	Total	Cadaver	Living
1980	4,697	3,422	1,275
1981	4,885	3,427	1,458
1982	5,358	3,681	1,677
1983	6,112	4,328	1,784
1984	6,968	5,264	1,704

On the one hand, the use of cadaver kidneys has been applauded because it avoids risks to the health of living donors and reduces risks of manipulation and coercion—for example, a family may put pressure on a reluctant donor to provide a kidney to another family member. On the other hand, a policy of not transplanting kidneys from competent living donors has been opposed as unwarranted paternalism because such a donor's decision may be adequately informed and voluntary. In a fuller examination of these issues, it is useful to distinguish genetically related from genetically unrelated donors.

Living Related Donors

In the past it was accurate to say that "donor grafts from siblings and parents show superior functional success over cadaver grafts."[44] But these sources could not meet the need for kidneys in the population: "eighty per cent of potential recipients have relatives who are unsuitable donors because of antigenic incompatibility, kidney disease, and renal anatomical problems."[45] Thus, living related donors are an insufficient source of kidneys for transplantation. However, the putative advantages of living related donor kidneys have now been challenged by Dr. Thomas Starzl, among others, because of the increasing survival rates of cadaver kidney grafts with cyclosporine.[46]

The major ethical concerns about living related donors who are competent to consent focus on their understanding of the risks and their willingness to undergo the surgical procedure and to accept the risks. Some studies show that family members frequently decide to donate a kidney when they hear that a relative needs one, even before they have been informed about the risks. Furthermore, such donors frequently use the language of "necessity" to describe their choice: "I could not have lived with myself if I had failed to donate," or "I had no choice."[47] Neither deciding before being informed about the risks nor experiencing donation as a necessity always invalidates the donor's consent. Donors may have decided that their reasons for donating (e.g., to save a relative's life) outweigh any risks, and their language of necessity may simply indicate the importance of their reasons for donation. Of course, judgments about the adequacy of a donor's understanding and voluntariness can only be made in the situation, and professionals need to be sensitive to inadequacies on any of these levels, perhaps especially to subtle signs of coercion from other members of the family. Physicians sometimes justifiably provide a "medical excuse" for potential donors under severe external pressure to donate.[48]

Two classes of living related donors are particularly controversial because their autonomy is severely limited and even nonexistent in some cases: children (especially preadolescent children) and mentally retarded persons. Because of the limitations on their capacity to give valid consent, it may be unjust to impose the burdens and risks of kidney removal on them in order to benefit some other member of the family.[49] The counterargument is that even though children and mentally retarded persons lack the capacity to give valid consent to organ removal, they can sometimes assent to (or dissent from) such a procedure, and, more importantly, they frequently derive significant nonmedical benefits from "organ donation."[50] These benefits may result, for example, from the survival of a family member who contributes greatly to the "donor's" well-being and happiness. There are reasons to be suspicious about such claims for such benefits in many cases, but it is not clear that all uses of children or mentally retarded persons as "organ donors" for other members of a family should be categorically prohibited as unjust. At the very least, there should be independent, judicial review of any proposal to remove an organ from an incompetent, dependent, and vulnerable person.[51] This review should determine whether the heavy presumption against using such a person as a "donor" can be rebutted because of significant nonmedical benefits to him or her in the absence of alternative means to save the recipient's life.

Living Unrelated Donors

There has been a clear trend away from using living unrelated donors. Prior to 1967, living unrelated donors provided 14.5 percent of the transplanted kidneys.[52] Since 1970 few kidneys have been obtained from living unrelated donors for transplantation. In addition to fear of medical malpractice suits, there appears to be suspicion of the motives of people who want to donate to strangers. However, the motives of such genetically unrelated donors as spouses and friends may be as altruistic as the motives of such genetically related donors as parents, children, or siblings. Decisions about their acceptability should be made on a case-by-case basis. At any rate, the use of prisoners as sources of kidneys in exchange for such special considerations as early parole constitutes exploitation of a captive and vulnerable population. It is not clear whether the use of several prisoners at a Colorado state penitentiary as sources of kidneys in the 1960s was exploitative;[53] but the moral risks are too great for such a practice perhaps even with the most rigorous safeguards. In addition, in view of reports of brokerage of kidneys from living unrelated sources, especially nonimmigrant aliens, the Task Force on Organ Transplantation has recommended that transplant centers demand objective proof of consanguinity and assign an advocate for the potential donor.[54]

SELECTION OF RECIPIENTS OF ORGAN TRANSPLANTS

Scarcity of organs for transplantation will probably remain a problem for the indefinite future; indeed, it is possible that the demand will always exceed the supply. Under these circumstances, there will be difficult questions concerning the process and criteria of patient selection.

The National Organ Transplant Act (PL 98–507) required the Task Force on Organ Transplantation to make "recommendations for assuring equitable access by patients to organ transplantation and for assuring the equitable allocation of donated organs among transplant centers and among patients medically qualified for an organ transplant."

Whatever the legal picture, which is not totally clear, it can be argued morally that donated organs belong to the public. This fundamental conviction undergirded the Task Force's deliberations and recommendations regarding equitable access to organ transplantation: donated organs should be viewed as scarce national resources to be used for the welfare of the community. Organ procurement and transplant teams receive donated organs as trustees and stewards for the community, and they determine who will receive available organs. The available evidence suggests that they generally make responsible decisions. However, because of some widely publicized exceptions, there is increasing demand that the public participate in formulating the criteria for patient selection in order to ensure that they are fair. This demand stems in part from the nature of the organ procurement system, which depends on voluntary gifts to strangers. Indeed, policies of organ procurement and policies of organ distribution interact. If policies of distribution are perceived to be unfair, policies of procurement may be ineffective because of public distrust.

Most conceptions of justice permit rationing or triage under conditions of scarcity, but they rule out selection criteria that are based on morally irrelevant characteristics, such as race or sex. The major debates focus on which characteristics are morally relevant and which are morally irrelevant in the two stages in the selection of patients for organ transplantation, (1) formation of a waiting list, and (2) distribution of available organs. There is general agreement that the waiting list of candidates for transplantation should be determined primarily by medical criteria: the need for and the probability of benefiting from an organ transplant. However, there is debate about whether these medical criteria should be drawn broadly or narrowly. Many believe that the fairest procedure is to use broad medical criteria to establish the waiting list and then to use narrower medical criteria to determine who should actually receive an available organ. In addition, there is debate about the specification and weight of different medical criteria, as well as about the medical relevance of such factors as age. While rejecting some criteria of access as unjust—for example, favoritism, bribery, sex discrimination, race discrimination, and ability to pay—the Task Force came to the conclusion that it is impossible and risky to try to close this debate about other criteria now. The debate should continue, with significant public input. This public process would be embodied in part in the proposed and urgently needed national Organ Procurement and Transplantation Network.[55]

Why employ both need and probability of success? They reflect medical utility, which requires the maximization of welfare among patients suffering from end-stage organ failure. Medical utility should not be confused with social utility, which focuses on the value of salvageable patients for society.[56] By contrast, medical utility requires that organs be used as effectively and as efficiently as possible to benefit as many patients as possible. For example, if there is no reasonable chance that a transplant will be successful for a particular patient, it would be poor stewardship to give the organ to that patient.

Judgments about medical need and probability of success are obviously value-laden. For example, there is debate about what will count as success—such as length of graft survival, length of patient survival, quality of life, rehabilitation—and about the factors that influence the probability of success. Some contraindications are well established, such as mismatched blood group or positive donor-recipient cross match. On the basis of current evidence, the Task Force argues that both medical utility and justice indicate that a recipient with zero mismatches for HLA-A, -B, and -DR antigens should be offered that organ and that O blood type organs should always be offered first to suitable O recipients.[57] However, there is debate about the relative importance of tissue matching now that cyclosporine is available, and this technical debate influences judgments about the conditions under which kidneys should be shared outside the location where they were retrieved. For example, since cyclosporine is nephrotoxic, a retrieved kidney needs to be transplanted sooner than usual in order to increase the chances of successful transplantation. Sometimes there is a tension between urgency of need and probability of success. For example, some members of a Canadian transplant team have written: "When determining who will get a heart, it becomes a difficult ethical issue as to whether the patient with the better outcome or the individual with the greatest urgency should receive the heart. The patients themselves would opt for the patient with the greatest urgency and by and large that is the decision taken by the team. However, one is conscious of the fact that one may be affecting the overall success rate by making choices in favour of individual patient urgency rather than making them on the basis of success."[58] Some argue that medical urgency should include not only the immediate threat of death but also the likelihood of not receiving another organ because of level of sensitization. Sensitized patients are those who, often as a result of a previous failed transplant or blood transfusions, have developed antibodies to many different human leukocyte antigens (HLA) and whose bodies would reject organs with those antigens. Sensitized patients now constitute a hard core of waiting lists for kidney transplantation. The Task Force recommends that a highly sensitized patient who is predicted either on the basis of computer antibody analysis or actual cross match to accept the transplant should be given priority over equivalently matched nonsensitized patients.[59] And yet the success rates are lower for sensitized patients than for nonsensitized patients.

If two or more patients are equally good candidates for a particular organ according to the medical criteria of need and probability of success, the principle of justice suggests that their time on the waiting list may be the fairest way to make the final selection.[60] How often this criterion of first-come, first-served is relevant will depend on how frequently a good HLA match or a compatible sensitized recipient becomes available to claim higher priority for the organ. If this is only 15 to 20 percent of the time, as some have estimated, most of the organs will need to be allocated on criteria other than HLA match and sensitization. The criterion of time on the waiting list would often give priority to highly sensitized patients over similarly matched nonsensitized patients.

Several other criteria have been proposed, and it is important to examine them carefully in order to make sure that they reflect medical utility rather than social utility and that they are not otherwise unfair. For example, former HHS Secretary Patricia Harris withdrew the earlier tentative authorization for Medicare to cover some heart transplants in part because of her concern that some criteria for patient selection were more social than medical.[61] Because judgments of social utility may be camouflaged as judgments of medical utility, it is essential that the criteria of patient selection be publicly developed and stated as well as fairly applied.

Among other possible criteria, age has sometimes been proposed. For example, the United Kingdom tends not to provide either dialysis or transplantation for people over sixty.[62] Several reasons have been offered for assigning priority to younger candidates. If increasing age correlates with a decline in the capacity to withstand operations and with an increase in other medical problems that reduce the probability of successful transplantation, age may be medically relevant. In addition, age could enter into the calculus if length of survival after transplantation is emphasized in medical utility. These first two reasons for assigning priority to younger candidates rest on medical utility—age as a predictor of successful outcome and a longer period of survival after transplantation. Such ethicists as Norman Daniels and Robert Veatch also argue that considerations of justice in the allocation of resources over the whole life span justify assigning priority to younger candidates over older candidates.[63] However, in view of the widespread controversy about the appropriateness of the criterion of age, it is important to exercise the utmost caution about its use in order to avoid unwarranted discrimination against older patients.

Second, some have argued that it is not unjust to assign low priority to transplant candidates whose life-styles brought on their problems (e.g., alcoholism resulting in liver disease).[64] However, such factors as social compassion and uncertainty about the connection between many life-styles and diseases militate against implementing such a policy. Furthermore, the life-styles themselves may not have been voluntarily chosen. In some cases, however, a behavioral pattern, such as alcoholism or drug addiction, may be medically relevant in determining the probability of successful transplantation. For example, a patient's continued heavy use of alcohol and drugs may greatly reduce the probability that a transplant will be successful, and neither medical utility nor justice requires that such a patient receive a transplant under conditions of scarcity.

Another controversial criterion of selection for organ transplantation is whether the patient has a social network of support. It can be argued that this criterion is medically relevant, because such a social network may increase the probability of a successful outcome, especially in rehabilitation. According to the Massachusetts Task Force on Organ Transplantation, "family support networks may be extremely important in after-hospital care," but "the absence of a family or the existence of an unconventional substitute should not serve as a reason to exclude the patient from evaluation." Instead, "society should develop mechanisms, in cooperation with the transplanting hospitals, to provide sufficient support resources for such patients during their recuperation," including the costs of aftercare in the analysis of the costs of the transplantation itself.[65]

Yet another possible criterion is whether a patient has already received one or more transplants. Between 1977 and 1981, 10,818 people received 11,615 kidney transplants, with 10,063 patients receiving one transplant, 713 receiving two, and 42 patients receiving three or more.[66] Although some analysts contend that equitable access to scarce organs for transplantation should limit a patient to one transplant, others resist this conclusion, holding that to deny the patient another transplant would constitute abandonment. Judgments may differ depending on whether there are backup or alternative treatments, such as dialysis for end stage renal disease.

Donors of organs usually give them to unidentified recipients without geographical restrictions and do not want those organs wasted. But do the location of donors and the location of recipients have any moral bearing, apart from technical and practical problems in sharing organs from one location to another? Some argue that the conviction that donated organs belong to the community and are thus public resources implies that "in principle, and to the extent technically and practically achievable, any citizen or resident of the U.S. in need of a transplant should be considered as a potential recipient of each retrieved organ on a basis equal to that of a patient who lives in the area where the organs or tissues are retrieved. Organs and tissues ought to be distributed on the basis of objective priority criteria, and not on the basis of accidents of geography."[67] Practical, technical, and even ethical limitations are still significant. If we could assume reciprocity—all centers would give and receive—location would appear to be morally irrelevant. Nevertheless, for the interim before an ideal system of sharing can be implemented, geographical factors are often emphasized, particularly when they reflect voluntary, cooperative systems of organ retrieval and distribution. For example, the report of the Massachusetts Task Force on Organ Transplantation holds that "Massachusetts has a special, historical relationship to our neighboring states, and that residents of the New England states that have been involved with the New England Organ Bank's program should be eligible for transplants on the same basis as Massachusetts citizens."[68] Outsiders would not be excluded altogether; they could be included on waiting lists if they were informed that priority would be given to New England residents. It is sometimes argued that using organs where they were donated provides an occasion for public education and increases the public's willingness to donate, as well as providing an incentive for the procurement team. However, it is unclear that these considerations would be very important in a system that involved full reciprocity.

In addition to the increased risk of damage to the retrieved organ through transportation and delay in transplantation, Dr. Olga Jonasson has argued that mandated sharing on the basis of HLA match (apart from the six antigen match or zero antigen mismatch) could actually be unfair to blacks and Hispanics. Most organ donors are white, certain HLA phenotypes are different in white, black, and Hispanic populations, and the identification of HLA phenotypes is less complete for blacks and Hispanics; thus, mandated sharing of retrieved organs according to HLA typing could reduce access of blacks and Hispanics to kidneys, even though they have a much higher rate of end stage renal disease (perhaps four to five times the rate of whites).[69]

After disclosures, especially by the *Pittsburgh Press*, that some nonresident, nonimmigrant aliens received priority over American citizens for scarce organs retrieved in the United States, a heated debate erupted about the boundaries of moral community for the distribution of organs. At Presbyterian Hospital in Pittsburgh on May 4, 1985, two cadaver kidneys became available from a fifteen-year-old North Carolina resident. The waiting list included a sixty-year-old American woman who had been on the list for three years, who had almost exhausted her bodily sites for hookup to dialysis machines, and whose organ-rejecting antibodies were at a lower level than usual and within acceptable limits for transplantation; an Egyptian physician's eleven year old son who had not yet been put on dialysis; and a Saudi Arabian who had only been in the United States seven weeks waiting for a transplant. The kidneys were used for the last two candidates.[70] In part the debate about such cases has focused on the relevance of a patient's ability to pay more than the federal government pays through the End-Stage Renal Disease (ESRD) Program. If money is the real reason for assigning priority to nonimmigrant aliens, or for shipping organs abroad, then the transplant institution is selling organs that have been donated to the community. However, in addition to this issue, which I will discuss in the next section, several other significant issues are involved in the debate about nonimmigrant aliens.

No moral considerations support giving nonimmigrant aliens priority for scarce organs retrieved in the United States from American citizens, but there are strong moral and other reasons for granting some nonimmigrant aliens access to organs retrieved in the United States. Total exclusion has been opposed as wasteful, unfair, and uncharitable. Regarding the argument from wastage, it is probable that wastage of kidneys could be reduced by increasing the number of American citizens on the waiting lists for kidney transplantation. Currently only 8,000 to 10,000 of the 75,000 patients on dialysis are also on waiting lists for transplantation. Total exclusion has also been opposed as chauvinistic; it neglects the international goodwill that American transplant programs can generate especially if they combine transplantation of some foreign na-- tionals with efforts to develop transplant programs in their countries.

Perhaps the most common argument for transplanting some nonimmigrant aliens is that medical humanitarianism does not recognize criteria of sex, race, nationality, and so forth. This humanitarianism appears to be reflected in the international laws of war, which require equal treatment of wounded enemy soldiers and wounded fellow soldiers. However, this requirement may be construed as an effort to ensure equal treatment for one's comrades when they fall into the hands of the enemy. After all, an occupying army is not similarly obligated by the laws of war to provide equal medical treatment to wounded civilians in occupied areas. According to this line of argument, there might be an obligation to share with foreign nationals whose countries participate in a reciprocal system. But it is difficult to find strong moral reasons to establish an obligation to transplant nonresident, nonimmigrant aliens from countries that refuse to participate in systems of giving and receiving organs. However, it may be generous and praiseworthy to do so, as long as the sacrifices are not excessive for citizens within the voluntary, cooperative system of organ procurement. After all, when it is impossible to meet the needs of everyone, it may be permissible to give priority to near neighbors (citizens) over distant neighbors.

Despite the widespread agreement that nonimmigrant aliens should not be totally excluded, there has been vigorous debate about which of two policies should be adopted: (1) accepting some nonimmigrant aliens on the waiting list after informing them that they would not receive an organ unless it was clear that no American could benefit from it, or (2) accepting a maximum number (perhaps 5 to 10 percent) of foreign nationals on the waiting list and treating them equally with American citizens (perhaps excluding them altogether from some categories of extreme scarcity or with long waiting lists, such as patients with O blood type).

The first policy would give American citizens priority for organs but would accept some nonimmigrant aliens at the bottom of the waiting list or on a separate (but unequal) waiting list. The major objection to this policy is that such patients are then treated as second-class patients, even if they voluntarily accept their position in order to have a slight chance for an organ. Indeed, some argue, this position is unfair because it leads nonimmigrant aliens to come to the United States in the false hope of a realistic opportunity to obtain an organ. In order to avoid such inequities, the second policy would accept a limited number of nonimmigrant aliens. Even if sharing with distant neighbors is an ideal, some limits are reasonable, and the figure of 10 percent has been developed in some religious and moral traditions that recognize a principle of tithing. Such a policy would probably be feasible, since public protest appears to have been directed against priority to nonimmigrant aliens, not against any sharing with nonimmigrant aliens. However, critics contend that any numerical limit is arbitrary and that this policy is still unfair to American citizens who should have priority over nonimmigrant aliens in the competition for scarce organs.

It is possible to develop one policy for renal organs and another for other organs. For example, it could be argued that the second policy is acceptable for kidneys because they are not as scarce as other organs and because dialysis is usually available as a backup or alternative treatment, while the first policy is acceptable for other organs. A similar compromise was reached by the federal Task Force, with anticipation of further review by the Organ Transplantation Network.[71]

PROVISION OF FUNDS FOR TRANSPLANTATION

Earlier it was noted that ability to pay was one criterion of patient selection rejected by the Task Force as unjust. Even with the best policies of procurement, organs are likely to remain scarce, and problems of access and allocation will continue to require some public policies for the distribution of retrieved organs. One fundamental question is whether the federal government should provide funds, perhaps as a last resort, for those who cannot pay for transplants in order to eliminate the criterion of ability to pay. Even if it is unfair to sell organs to the highest bidder, to the patient who can pay more than the going rate, there may still be debate about whether it is unfair to select the recipient who can pay the going rate.

Currently renal transplantation, along with dialysis, is covered by the ESRD Program of Medicare (Section 2291 of PL 92-603, which became effective October 30, 1972) for practically all patients who need renal transplantation regardless of their finances. The costs are tremendous—over $3 billion each year for approximately 75,000 patients. However, the patients receiving dialysis now more nearly reflect the incidence of end stage renal disease among the population than the patients who were selected for dialysis in the late sixties and early seventies. At that time priority was clearly given to white, college-educated males; now society's provision of funds has resulted in more equal access.[72]

In addition, cornea transplants, some bone marrow transplants, and some liver transplants for children are covered by the Health Care Financing Administration (HCFA). After extensive review of heart transplantation by the HCFA in light of the massive Battelle Institute study, Medicare coverage has been extended to a limited number of heart transplants. (As noted above, an earlier tentative authorization for Medicare to cover heart transplants was withdrawn in 1980.) Medicaid coverage varies from state to state; more than half do not pay for heart and liver transplants, some pay for liver but not heart transplants, some make a case-by-case determination, and some have no policies. Most reimburse for kidney transplants. It has been estimated that approximately 80 percent of commercial insurers and Blue Cross and Blue Shield plans now cover both heart and liver transplants.[73]

PL 98-507 instructed the Task Force on Organ Transplantation to make an assessment, prior to its final report, of immunosuppressive therapies, including "an analysis of the comparative advantages of grants, coverage under existing Federal programs, or other means to assure that individuals who need such [immunosuppressive] medications can obtain them." This is an important issue in part because cyclosporine is so expensive (approximately $6,000 a year for kidney transplant recipients) and because the ESRD program does not cover outpatient medications. The Task Force found that approximately 25 percent of the transplant population had no coverage of immunosuppressive therapies through private insurance programs or state programs, including Medicaid, and that the inability to pay for these medications had become a factor in the selection of patients for transplantation. The Task Force recommended the establishment of a joint Health Care Financing Administration–Public Health Service (HCFA-PHS) program "to provide immunosuppressive medications to transplant centers for distribution to financially needy Medicaid eligible transplant patients."[74] This recommendation was designed to eliminate inequities based on inability to pay for immunosuppressive therapies. At that time the Task Force made no recommendation regarding the funding of extrarenal transplants themselves until it could gain sufficient information and carefully consider the issues involved. Its final report recommends that the federal government, as a last resort, ensure equitable access to all transplants that are efficacious and cost-effective. Several arguments support this recommendation.

The first argument rests on *a societal obligation to ensure every citi-*

zen equitable access to a decent minimum or an adequate level of health care. Such an argument usually appeals to moral principles of social compassion and justice in response to health care needs.[75] Health crises are often viewed as random and unpredictable results of natural lottery. The society's obligation to meet those health needs may stem from its sense of justice (e.g., those needs are unfair) or its sense of compassion (e.g., those needs are unfortunate). The President's Commission for the Study of Ethical Problems in Biomedical and Behavioral Research held that a standard of "equitable access to health care requires that all citizens be able to secure an adequate level of care without excessive burdens."[76] Major difficulties emerge in specifying "an adequate level of care" and "excessive burdens." In view of these difficulties the President's Commission held that these standards should be specified through "fair, democratic political procedures." Debates about whether organ transplantation should be part of the decent minimum of health care, which the society is obligated to provide, tend to focus on what is required for an adequate level of health care. Important tests of adequacy include (1) the nature of the health needs in question—for example, whether they are life-threatening, (2) whether the health care in question offers a reasonable chance of meeting those needs, and (3) whether the probable benefits outweigh the probable costs. The claim that some organ transplants are experimental rather than established—and thus are not part of a decent minimum or an adequate level of health care— focuses primarily on (2) with some attention to (3). However, some extrarenal organ transplants are both efficacious and cost-effective. For example, according to the Battelle Institute study, heart transplants appear to satisfy the above tests and should be construed as part of the decent minimum or adequate level of health care. Critics of this first argument contend that drawing lines is difficult if not impossible—for example, between heart transplantation and the artificial heart—but defenders insist that it is possible to draw lines on the basis of the above three tests.

A second argument rests on *the precedent society created in funding (1) several areas of health care, or specifically, (2) renal transplantation.* Because society has chosen to end wealth discrimination in several areas of health care, including kidney transplantation in the ESRD Program, it should also end wealth discrimination in extrarenal transplants, if they are efficacious and cost-effective. Critics would respond that it is not sufficient to appeal to this social precedent since there needs to be an independent argument that the precedent itself is defensible. Most defenses of the precedent appeal to a version of the first argument. Here again there are difficult questions of line-drawing, particularly since many people who do not qualify for indigent care cannot afford extrarenal transplants.

A third argument focuses directly on organ transplantation: *it is unfair and even exploitative for society to ask people to donate organs if those organs will then be distributed on the basis of ability to pay.* Whatever is claimed about the rest of health care, there is an independent argument for society to ensure equitable access to organs without regard for ability to pay. This argument connects organ procurement and distribution, and it appeals to what society does in procuring organs rather than to what society should do or already does in distributing other forms of health care including renal transplants. The system fails to meet the standards of justice when it solicits organs from all people for the community at large and then excludes some people, that is, those who cannot pay, from access to donated organs. This argument offers an independent justification for the societal funding of organ transplants, without building on a general right to health care or on what society already covers. It also does not raise difficult questions of line-drawing (e.g., heart transplantation versus the artificial heart) because of its focus on organ procurement and distribution. However, additional arguments are also relevant, particularly those showing that some extrarenal transplants are efficacious and cost-effective. Many are rightly concerned about the costs of health care, but the burden of saving public health funds should be distributed equitably rather than imposed on particular groups of patients, such as those suffering from end stage heart or liver failure.

If any or all of these arguments support a societal obligation to provide funds for organ transplants that are efficacious and cost-effective, there is still a question about which institutions should have primary responsibility for discharging this obligation. When the President's Commission held that there is a "societal obligation" to provide equitable access to health care, it referred to "society in the broadest sense—the collective American community," which consists of "individuals, who are in turn members of many other overlapping groups, both public and private; local, state, regional, and national units; professional and workplace organizations; religious, educational, and charitable organizations; and family, kinship, and ethnic groups." [77] Within this pluralistic approach, the President's Commission admitted a significant role for the federal government as the institution of last resort; it held that the "ulti-

mate responsibility" rests with the federal government "for seeing that
health care is available to all when the market, private charity, and government efforts at the state and local level are insufficient in achieving
equity."

If the moral arguments are sufficient to establish a societal obligation
to provide funds for organ transplantation, they also support a major
role for the federal government, at least in the last resort. Thus, the Task
Force on Organ Transplantation holds that the federal government
should ensure that each citizen has equitable access to organ transplantation through the provision of financial resources if necessary.[78] It is
unlikely that the Task Force's recommendation regarding societal and
governmental provision of funds will be implemented in the near future.
And the debate can be expected to continue about this question, as well
as about other criteria for patient selection and about policies to increase the supply of organs, as organ transplantation itself continues to
develop and expand.

NOTES

1. In this essay I have drawn heavily on materials I prepared for the deliberations and report of the national Task Force on Organ Transplantation (of which I was a member and vice-chairman), especially in the sections on patient selection and provision of funds for transplantation. I am grateful to the other members of the Task Force and to the Office of Organ Transplantation for numerous insights. In some other sections, especially the sections on living donors and the sale of organs, I used some paragraphs with revisions from my article "The Gift of Life: Ethical Problems and Policies in Obtaining and Distributing Organs for Transplantation," *Critical Care Clinics* 2 (Jan. 1986). 133–48. The overall structure and content appeared in an article prepared for *Biolaw*, vol. 1, *Research Manual*, 1986. I am grateful to the editors of the last two publications for permission to use these articles with revisions. In addition, I benefited greatly from discussions of these ideas at several institutions and conferences, particularly the Wilson Center, where Sen. Albert Gore, William May, and Arthur Caplan were the primary respondents, the University of North Carolina, the Catholic University School of Law, the Hastings Center, Juniata College, Emory and Henry College, and, of course, Southern Illinois University. This essay was completed in June 1986 and does not reflect developments after that time.

2. These statistics were developed by the Office of Organ Transplantation from several sources and appear in the final report of the federal Task Force on Organ Transplantation, *Organ Transplantation*.

3. See, for example, *Report of the Massachusetts Task Force on Organ Transplantation*.

4. Council on Scientific Affairs, "Organ Donor Recruitment."

5. Uniform Anatomical Gift Act, Secs. 2–4 (1968).

6. *U.S. Public's Attitudes Toward Organ Transplants*. See Appendix.

7. "Most in U.S. Found Willing to Donate Organs."

8. Kaufman et al., "Kidney Donation"; Stuart, Veith, and Cranford, "Brain Death Laws and Patterns of Consent."

9. The legal history in this paragraph has been drawn from T. D. Overcast and K. J. Merrikin, "Legal Issues Surrounding the Donor," in Evans et al., *National Heart Transplantation Study*, vol. 4, ch. 33.

10. *Holland v. Metalious*.

11. Prottas, "Encouraging Altruism," p. 284.

12. See, e.g., Titmuss, *Gift Relationship*; Simmons and Klein, *Gift of Life*; Fox and Swazey, *Courage to Fail*.

13. For a rich discussion of gifts, see Mauss, *Gift*, which is used but not fully reflected in several contemporary interpretations of organ transfer.

14. See Ramsey, *Patient as Person*; May, "Religious Justifications for Donating Body Parts"; Rosner and Bleich, eds., *Jewish Bioethics*.

15. *U.S. Public's Attitudes Toward Organ Transplants*.

16. For a similar list of values, see *Ethical, Legal and Policy Issues Pertaining to Solid Organ Procurement*.

17. However, in the Gallup Poll conducted in 1983 for the National Heart Transplantation Study, only 43.9 percent responded affirmatively to the question "Do you feel that

the next-of-kin should be allowed to donate the organs of relatives who have recently died but have not signed an organ donor card?" Manninen and Evans, "Public Attitudes and Behavior Regarding Organ Donation."

18. *U.S. Public's Attitudes Toward Organ Transplants.* See also Callender et al., "Attitudes Among Blacks Toward Donating Kidneys."

19. Ramsey, *Patient as Person.*

20. Caplan, "Organ Procurement."

21. In one major medical center that had averaged six organ donors per year, a policy of required request increased the number of organ donations to twenty in only nine months. Oh and Uniewski, "Enhancing Organ Recovery."

22. Task Force on Organ Transplantation, *Organ Transplantation.*

23. Stuart, Veith, and Cranford, "Brain Death Laws and Patterns of Consent."

24. Muyskens, "An Alternative Policy for Obtaining Cadaver Organs."

25. Simmons, "Tacit Consent and Political Obligations."

26. Ramsey, *Patient as Person.*

27. Prottas, "Organ Procurement in Europe and the United States."

28. Caplan, "Organ Procurement."

29. Denise, "Regulating the Sale of Human Organs."

30. Steinbrook, "Kidneys for Transplantation."

31. Titmuss, *Gift Relationship.*

32. Quoted in *Report of the Massachusetts Task Force on Organ Transplantation,* p. 101.

33. G. I. Mavrodes, "The Morality of Selling Human Organs," in *Ethics, Humanism, and Medicine,* ed. Basson.

34. Ibid.; Perry, "Human Organs and the Open Market."

35. Ramsey, *Patient as Person*; Dickens, "Control of Living Body Materials"; *National Organ Transplant Act: Hearings.*

36. *National Organ Transplant Act: Hearings,* pp. 125 and 130 (testimony of Cong. Albert Gore, Jr.).

37. Childress, "Implications of Major Western Religious Traditions for Policies Regarding Human Biological Materials."

38. See H.R. 540, 98th Cong., 1st Sess. (1983), which was not enacted.

39. Ramsey, *Patient as Person*; May, "Religious Justifications for Donating Body Parts."

40. *Head v. Colloton and Filer.* See also Lansing, "Conflict of Patient Privacy and The Freedom of Information Act"; Burt, "Coercion and Communal Morality"; Caplan et al., "Mrs. X and the Bone Marrow Transplant."

41. *McFall v. Shimp.* See also Meisel and Roth, "Must a Man Be His Cousin's Keeper?"

42. Kaufman et al., "Kidney Donation."

43. Task Force on Organ Transplantation, *Organ Transplantation.*

44. Berstein, "Organ Donor."

45. Kaufman et al., "Kidney Donation."

46. Starzl, "Will Live Organ Donations No Longer Be Justified?" Contrast Levey, Hou, and Bush, Jr., "Kidney Transplantation from Unrelated Living Donors."

47. Eisendrath, Guttmann, and Murray, "Psychologic Considerations in the Selection of Kidney Transplant Donors"; Fellner and Marshall, "Kidney Donors."

48. Bernstein, "Organ Donor."

49. Ramsey, *Patient as Person*.

50. Bernstein and Simmons, "Adolescent Kidney Donor"; Fost, "Children as Renal Donors"; Hollenberg, "Altruism and Coercion." Court decisions permitting organ removal from an incompetent for a relative include *Strunk v. Strunk* and *Little v. Little*. In the former the source of the kidney was an institutionalized twenty-seven-year-old man with an I.Q. of approximately 35. Court decisions against removal of a kidney from an incompetent source to benefit a relative include *Lausier v. Pescinski* and *In re* Richardson. For an analysis of the major cases, see Robertson, "Organ Donations by Incompetents," and Schwartz, "Bioethical and Legal Considerations," pp. 424–27.

51. Robertson, "Organ Donations by Incompetents."

52. Katz and Capron, *Catastrophic Disease*.

53. Steinbrook, "Kidneys for Transplantation"; Ramsey, *Patient as Person*.

54. Task Force on Organ Transplantation, *Organ Transplantation*.

55. Ibid.

56. For this distinction between medical utility and social utility, see Childress, "Triage in Neonatal Intensive Care."

57. Task Force on Organ Transplantation, *Organ Transplantation*.

58. Stiller, McKenzie, and Jostuk, "Cardiac Transplantation."

59. Task Force on Organ Tranplantation, *Organ Transplantation*.

60. Ramsey in *Patient as Person* argues for first-come, first-served as an "ongoing lottery," which is justified by several principles. Others also argue for the moral relevance and priority of queuing over judgments of social worth; see Childress, "Who Shall Live When Not All Can Live?" and Winslow, *Triage and Justice*. The *Report of the Massachusetts Task Force on Organ Transplantation* also recommends ranking patients according to their time on the waiting list. For the counterarguments, see Rescher, "Allocation of Exotic Lifesaving Medical Therapy," and Basson, "Choosing Among Candidates for Scarce Medical Resources." For other references, see Winslow, *Triage and Justice*, and Childress, "Rationing of Medical Treatment."

61. Knox, "Heart Transplants."

62. Wing, "Why Don't the British Treat More Patients with Kidney Failure?" p. 1157; Parsons and Lock, "Triage and the Patient with Renal Failure."

63. Daniels, *Just Health Care*; Veatch, ed., *Values and Life-extending Technologies*.

64. Veatch, "Voluntary Risks to Health."

65. *Report of the Massachusetts Task Force on Organ Transplantation*.

66. Office of Organ Transplantation, *Organ Transplantation Background Information*.

67. Council of the American Society of Transplant Physicians, testimony before the Task Force on Organ Transplantation.

68. *Report of the Massachusetts Task Force on Organ Transplantation*, p. 17.

69. Task Force on Organ Transplantation, *Organ Transplantation*.

70. Schneider and Flaherty, "Woman Passed Over."

71. Task Force on Organ Transplantation, *Organ Transplantation*.

72. Evans, Blagg, and Bryan, "Implications for Health Policy."

73. Health Insurance Association of America, *Organ Transplants*; Task Force on Organ Transplantation, *Report to the Secretary and the Congress on Immunosuppressive Therapies*, p. 44.

74. Task Force on Organ Transplantation, *Report to the Secretary and the Congress on Immunosuppressive Therapies.*

75. Childress, "Rights to Health Care in a Democratic Society."

76. President's Commission for the Study of Ethical Problems in Medicine and Biomedical and Behavioral Research, *Securing Access to Health Care.*

77. Ibid.

78. Task Force on Organ Transplantation, *Organ Transplantation.*

Appendix
Gallup Opinion Polls Regarding Organ Donation
Summary (by percentages)

	1968	1983 (Kidneys)	1985 (Organs generally)
Own	70	24 very likely 16 somewhat (31 say have signed donor cards)	24 very likely 18 somewhat (36 say have signed donor cards) (62 wouldn't mind if others donated)
Family		72 very likely 11 somewhat	71 very likely (Wishes of relative known) 14 somewhat
Child		50 very likely 16 somewhat	44 very likely 21 somewhat

Reasons (by percentages) identified as very important for not wanting to give permission for the use of one's own organs

	1983	1985
Premature action before really dead	15	23
Doctors might hasten death	11	21
Don't like to think about dying	15	18
Don't like idea of being cut up	20	16
Never really thought about it	20	14
Resurrection or afterlife	11	12
Others in family would object	10	10
Against my religion	7	9
Complicated to give permission	7	8

6

Terrorism and Moral Rights
Carl Wellman

It is sometimes thought, indeed it is often said, that the only plausible justifications of terrorism are utilitarian. One can imagine circumstances such that an act or series of acts of terrorism would, in spite of the obvious and regrettable harms they cause, produce much greater benefits in the long run. It might be that terrorism is the most effective means available to produce a social revolution that would be highly beneficial for the masses or the only practical means of ending the despotic rule of a foreign power imposing massive harms upon a colonial population. In such cases, one can plausibly argue that terrorism is morally justified because the benefits it achieves outweigh, even greatly outweigh, the harms it imposes upon its victims. But any such purely utilitarian justification completely ignores rights. If one takes individual rights seriously, moral philosophers frequently argue, then, it is obvious that terrorism is unjustified in each and every instance. One who admits that human beings have basic moral rights and recognizes that these impose side-constraints upon human conduct too strong to be overridden by a net balance of benefits over harms must, to be consistent, deny the possibility of any moral justification of terrorism no matter what the circumstances. Terrorism is the use or attempted use of terror as a means of coercion. Since the essential end of terrorism is coercion and its defining means the use of terror created by actual or threatened harm, terrorism by its very nature violates the moral rights to freedom, property, security of the person and even life of its victims. Hence, taking rights seriously rules out any justification of terrorism. Is this so?

To answer this question, consider some of the ways in which moral rights bear upon any possible justification, or condemnation, of terrorism. To avoid a treatment so abstract as to have no practical relevance at all, it will be useful to have some concrete examples of terrorism before our minds. Let us reflect together upon the antiabortion terrorism that has taken place recently in our own country. *Newsweek* of January 7, 1985, reported one revealing episode.

> Last June the Ladies Center, the only abortion clinic in Pensacola, Fla., was demolished by a still unsolved predawn bombing. At 3:23 on Christmas morning, vigilantes struck again, detonating a bomb in the new Ladies Center offices near Pensacola Regional Airport. Within 22 minutes, bombs also exploded in the offices of two local gynecologists who perform some abortions. Although no one was injured in the blasts, the offices of Dr. William Permenter were gutted by fire and the three explosions did an estimated $375,000 in damage. Permenter later said he would no longer perform in-office abortions and complained that no one would rent to him because of the insurance risk. But another victim, Dr. Bo Bagenholm, declared, "This isn't going to stop anything." [1]

Whether or not it is always morally wrong to violate someone's legal rights, it seems necessarily true that it is morally wrong to violate anyone's moral rights. If the report in *Newsweek* is accurate, one can hardly doubt that in this instance the terrorists did violate the rights to property of many individuals. What is usually spoken of as "the right to property" is highly complex. To simplify our discussion, let us consider only the owner's moral claim-right that others not destroy or damage his or her property. Here the owners of the Ladies Center had their original building, together with its contents, destroyed, and their new building was subsequently destroyed or severely damaged by the terrorists. The two gynecologists presumably owned medical equipment, and possibly office equipment also, that was destroyed or damaged when their offices were gutted by fire. The owner or owners of the office building suffered considerable damage to their property. Moreover, if they were coerced into refusing to rent to gynecologists, as Dr. Permenter alleged, then they suffered additional monetary damages because they now have a reduced number of potential renters so that the market value of their property has been reduced. Finally, the many patients whose medical records were destroyed or damaged through the bombings have had their claim-rights that others not damage or destroy their property violated. (Whatever the legal situation, morally speaking it seems that the patient owns, perhaps jointly with his or her physician and/or medical facility, his or her medical records. This property right is commonly recognized by the transfer of these records, upon request, whenever the patient changes physicians.) Since these acts of terrorism have thus violated important moral property rights of so many persons, it would seem that they must be morally unjustified.

But this conclusion does not necessarily follow. The terrorists, or their advocates, might reply that no property rights have been violated because the victims of the bombings had forfeited their moral rights to any and all property destroyed or damaged. The physicians who have performed abortions at the Ladies Center or in their offices have murdered many innocent unborn children and have thereby forfeited their moral rights to the property they have used in their grossly immoral practices. The owners of the Ladies Center have knowingly used their building and its contents to aid and abet these murderers and, as accomplices in grave moral wrongdoing, have also forfeited their rights to this property. Although the owners of the office building may not have known that the two gynecologists used their premises for murderous purposes, they could and should have known this and hence are morally implicated as persons who have aided and abetted Doctors Permenter and Bagenholm in many murders. The many patients who consulted physicians with the intention of obtaining abortions have incited to murder and have used their medical records in this immoral pursuit of a deadly goal. Granted that many valuable possessions have been destroyed or damaged, it does not follow that anyone's moral property rights have been violated because the possessors have forfeited their moral claims that others not destroy or damage their property by their immoral use of these possessions.

It is not clear whether this reply is adequate to meet the charge that important property rights have been violated. Let us assume, for the sake of discussion, that whenever one uses one's property in a grossly immoral action, one thereby forfeits one's moral rights to the property so misused. What of one's other property? Presumably one does not forfeit in addition one's moral rights to such untainted property. "One part-time counselor at an Alabama clinic came home to find her cat had been decapitated." [2] Surely she had not used her cat in any way in her activity of counseling pregnant women to have abortions. Thus, even granted that she had often recommended abortions and that this activity was grossly immoral (debatable assertions), her cat remained untainted by her wrongful action and, consequently, the killing of her cat constituted a violation of her moral claim that others not destroy her property. Similar observations are applicable to the Florida terrorism. Although the gynecologists who practiced at the Ladies Center and in their office did perform abortions, this was only a part of their practice. Much of their medical equipment was used for innocent purposes, some even to prevent spontaneous abortions. How can it be claimed that they have forfeited their moral rights to this untainted portion of their property? Since much of this was destroyed or damaged by the bombings, to this extent the terrorists have violated their property rights.

Another complication arises from the fact that some of the victims of the antiabortion terrorism seem to be entirely innocent parties. "The explosion that ripped through the Hillcrest Women's Surgi-Center in Washington, D.C., last week shattered 230 windows in two nearby apartment buildings."[3] Since neither the owners of these apartment buildings nor the tenants who rented or leased apartments in them were directly involved in any wrongful activities of the nearby Surgi-Center, unless a few of them happened to be employed there, they are innocent of the alleged murders against which the terrorists were directing their attacks. Accordingly, their property rights were not forfeited and the damage of their property was a violation of their moral rights. Again, most of the patients of the Ladies Center or of Doctors Permenter or Bagenholm had no intention of obtaining abortions. They sought medical advice or treatment in order to assure a healthy pregnancy or to maintain their health as female patients requiring the care of a gynecologist. Since they had not used their medical records in any way to incite their physicians to perform murderous abortions, they had not forfeited their moral property rights to their records. Thus, the destruction of or damage to their records must have been a violation of their moral rights. Since antiabortion bombing seems inevitably indiscriminate both by destroying or damaging untainted property and by wronging innocent parties, it seems impossible to justify it by claiming that no important property rights have been violated.

So be it. The defender of antiabortion terrorism can try to rebut the argument that such terrorism is necessarily unjustified because it violated important property rights in another manner. In this tragic situation, there is a conflict between the moral right to property of innocent parties and the right to life of the innocent human fetuses. Since the latter takes precedence over the former, the terrorism in question is morally justified even though it may, indirectly, violate property rights. Of course, just why one moral right overrides another needs to be explained. Presumably the explanation is not that rights to mere property are less important than or on a lesser moral level than rights of the person. Rights *to* property are equally rights *of* persons. A more plausible explanation is that life is a necessary condition of the exercise or enjoyment of any right whatsoever. Hence, the right to life necessarily takes first place in any weighing of the conflicting claims of any set of rights. It follows that antiabortion terrorism is justified by the way in which it protects the right to life of the fetus, a right that takes precedence over any conflicting right such as the right to property.

Even if the right to life does take precedence over every other right, this principle may be inapplicable to the justification of antiabortion terrorism. Such acts of terrorism can protect the right to life of the fetus only if abortion, the act of causing the death of the fetus, violates, or at the very least threatens to violate, the right to life of the fetus. But the fetus, even the human fetus, may not have any moral right to life simply because it is not the sort of being that can meaningfully be said to be a right-holder. No one condemns a physician who removes a mole from a mother's face on the grounds that this is a violation of the mole's moral right to life. Moles and warts, even human moles and warts, are simply not the kinds of entities that can be said to possess rights. Many philosophers maintain that only a person, or a moral agent, or a rational being is capable of possessing rights. Since the human fetus lacks personality, agency, and the capacity to reason, it is arguably incapable of having any moral rights at all. If this is so, then the terrorist's appeal to the right to life of the fetus fails to rebut the charge that antiabortion bombings are morally unjustified because they violate important property rights.

At this point there are a number of plausible replies available to anyone who wishes to defend the morality of antiabortion terrorism. One could propose some different criterion for the capacity to possess moral rights. If what is necessary and sufficient to be a right-holder is being alive or being created in the image of God, then the human fetus might well possess a right to life. The difficulty, of course, is defending one's chosen criterion. One could, instead, point out that there are very different species of rights. Granted that personality or moral agency or the capacity to reason are required for the possession of liberty-rights or power-rights, for these can be exercised only through the actions of the right-holder, these features are not necessary for the possession of claim-rights, for these are enjoyed when the duty-bearers upon whom they impose correlative moral obligations act as they ought to act. Since the right to life is the claim-right not to have one's life taken by another, the fetus may well be capable of possessing this sort of right. The difficulty here is that this presupposes that the language of rights is radically ambiguous so that there are quite different criteria for the application of the expression "a moral right" in different sorts of contexts. Hence, the most typical reply at this point is an appeal to the potentialities of the human fetus. Although the fetus does not actually possess personality, moral agency, or the capacity to reason, it *now* possesses the potentiality for all three, and this potentiality—a potentiality lacking in the feline fetus or even a full-grown cat —now confers upon the human fetus those rights possessed by the normal adult human being.

Disagreements about whether the human fetus is the sort of being that is capable of possessing moral rights are exceedingly complex and raise a number of highly controversial issues. Since the theory of rights has yet to provide any adequate basis for a rational resolution of these disagreements, let us avoid lengthy and unprofitable debate by granting the terrorist's thesis that moral rights can meaningfully be ascribed to beings who possess the relevant human capacities potentially. On this assumption, we must grant also that the human fetus does have a moral right to life. Still, it remains true that being a potential person, moral agent, or rational being is being significantly less than an actual person, moral agent or rational being. The moral rights of the fetus, therefore, have less moral weight than the rights of the mother. Accordingly, the mother's right to choose overrides the right to life of the fetus, and antiabortion terrorism is morally unjustified because it violates the greater right in its attempts to protect the lesser right. More specifically, such terrorism violates the mother's right to choose whether to carry the fetus to term or to have an abortion. Since this choice so profoundly affects her life, it is her choice and she has the right to make and act on it. Just as no woman ought morally to be forced to marry against her will, so no woman ought to be forced to deliver a child against her will.

The defender of antiabortion terrorism will no doubt reply that one misrepresents the moral situation if one describes it as involving a conflict between the right to life of the fetus and the right to choose of the mother. There is no moral right to choose to have an abortion. No doubt a woman does have a right to make many, even most, decisions that fundamentally affect her life, such as the choice of whether to remain single or to marry, but she does not have any moral right to choose whether to remain pregnant or have an abortion because to choose the latter is to choose to be an accomplice in murder. Compare the moral situation of a woman who finds herself trapped in an unhappy, even a brutal, marriage. Surely the wife has a moral right to choose whether to remain living with her husband or to separate from him; most of us would add that she has a right to choose to obtain a divorce. But no matter how much her marriage threatens her happiness, her career, even her physical well-being, she has no right to choose to murder her husband. This solution to her predicament is not morally permissible. Since murder is morally wrong, there can be no moral right to murder. Hence, there can be no moral right to choose to murder—or to incite to murder, either. Choosing to have an abortion is choosing to incite one's physician to murder one's unborn child. Therefore, the mother has no moral right to choose an abortion.

Is the alleged right to choose to have an abortion genuine? Yes, because it is implied by the acknowledged human right to privacy on which it is grounded. Article 12 of the Universal Declaration of Human Rights reads in part: "No one shall be subjected to arbitrary interference with his privacy." [4] Although this document is not above criticism, it does represent something approaching a consensus and should be treated with respect. It seems to me that there is a fundamental moral right to privacy and what is problematic is only its definition. It seems to me that the right to privacy is the moral claim-right that others not intrude into the private areas of one's life. This right is violated by unreasonable searching of my house, by tapping my private telephone without my permission, or by filming my acts of sexual intercourse without my knowledge. Broadcasting recordings of my telephone conversations or showing films of my sex life to my fascinated students also counts as intruding into these private areas.

A more recently recognized area of privacy is constituted by the sphere of private decisions. The recalcitrant problem is to explain what it is that makes any decision private so that interference by others is morally impermissible. The traditional "no harm to others" principle it seems to me is implausible. Almost every act one might perform, and therefore almost any decision one might make, will affect others in various ways—some of them harmful. If private decisions are those that do not harm others in any way, then the zone of private decisions will be limited to the most trivial of decisions, so trivial as to call for no fundamental human right to privacy.

It is much more plausible to define a private decision as one that fundamentally affects one's life for better or worse and does not so fundamentally affect the lives of any others. On this criterion, the abortion decision—the decision whether to remain pregnant or to have an abortion—is a private decision of the mother. This decision will affect her life fundamentally for better or worse and will not affect the life of any other individual, even her sexual partner, in a similarly profound manner. But what of the fetus? The decision to have an abortion does not affect the life of the fetus for better or worse because until a human being becomes conscious, it does not have a life that has intrinsic value, either positive or negative. Accordingly, the abortion decision really is a private decision that falls within the scope of the human right to privacy. Therefore, the mother's right to choose to have an abortion is a genuine moral right.

This derivation of a right to choose to have an abortion from the alleged human right to privacy could be taken as a *reductio ad absurdum* of the right to privacy. If choosing to incite to murder really is a private decision, then there surely can be no moral right to privacy. More likely, one who wanted to justify antiabortion terrorism would challenge this derivation. The right to privacy can be granted and its importance acknowledged while at the same time one insists that its scope is limited. Does the husband's right to privacy really rule out intrusions into the privacy of his home to interfere with his acts of battering his wife? Does the mother's right to make and act on private decisions, decisions that fundamentally affect her life, imply any claim-right that others not interfere with her choice of infanticide if it appears to her that this is necessary in order for her to pursue her career, a career basic to her entire life plan?

No one can plausibly pretend that the human right to privacy is absolute and unlimited. Even the Universal Declaration prohibits only "arbitrary interference" with one's privacy. Interference to prevent murder is far from arbitrary; indeed, it is called for by the moral law. If the moral law is to serve one of its essential functions, the protection of the moral rights of potential victims of wrongdoing, then each and every moral agent must have a moral right, perhaps even a moral duty, to enforce the moral law even when this involves intruding into the lives of others and interfering with their wrongful decisions. Since antiabortion terrorism serves to enforce the moral law in a way that helps to protect the moral rights of the fetus, it is morally justified.

This attempted justification calls to mind a famous passage from chapter two of Locke's *Second Treatise of Civil Government:*

> And that all men may be restrained from invading others' rights, and from doing hurt to one another, and the law of nature be observed . . . the execution of the law of nature is in that state put into every man's hand, whereby every one has a right to punish the transgressors of that law to such a degree as may hinder its violation.[5]

This passage refers exclusively, however, to individuals living in a state of nature. In a state of society, private citizens have no such right.

Private initiative is no longer necessary when officials are legally authorized to protect the rights of the citizens and punish wrongdoers. Indeed, an orderly and just political society is possible only if individuals
limit their natural right to use force and agree to abide by laws imposed
upon them by their duly authorized sovereign. Thus, within a society,
only an officer of the court may imprison a thief or execute a murderer,
and then only after a fair trial and legal conviction. *Newsweek* quite
properly reported that "At 3:23 on Christmas morning, vigilantees
struck again." [6] Antiabortion terrorism in our society constitutes one
form of vigilantism, and such actions violate the legal rights to liberty
and security of the person—sometimes even life—of its victims. It is
not merely that vigilantism is illegal; it is morally wrong because every
citizen has a moral right that all fellow citizens respect his or her legal
rights. One cannot justify antiabortion terrorism by any appeal to the
right to enforce the moral law. To be sure, even in a society, every moral
agent has a right to judge the conduct of others as morally right or
wrong, to disapprove wrongdoing and to censure the wrongdoer publicly. But this falls short of any right to enforce morality, for in a state of
society the use of force is reserved, with very few exceptions, to officials legally authorized to protect rights and punish wrongdoing.

At this point, one might well object that this condemnation of antiabortion terrorism illegitimately confuses the legal and moral points of
view. Legal rights and duties are one thing; moral rights and duties quite
another. One cannot assume any necessary connection between the two.
It may be true that each and every citizen has a legal right that every
fellow citizen respect his or her legal rights to liberty, security of person, and life. No doubt this does imply a legal duty of antiabortionists
to refrain from acts of terrorism that would violate these rights. But this
does not imply any corresponding moral duty. Nor can this logical gap
be filled by appealing to any moral right of the citizen that all fellow
citizens respect his or her legal rights. Although the terrorists and the
victim may be fellow citizens in their legal community, they are not fellow members in a moral community.

Physicians who regularly perform abortions are serial murderers, and
such mass murderers are moral outlaws. I am using the word "outlaw"
here in a very special sense analogous to the legal term "outlaw" when
"used in the sense that he has put himself beyond the pale of the law and
forfeited its protection, as in the case of a fugitive from justice for
whom proclamation has been made and who may be slain, if he refuses
to surrender, by any citizen without accusation or impeachment of

crime." [7] While a moral criminal, say someone who has wrongfully destroyed property, may have forfeited his or her right to property, a moral outlaw, such as a mass murderer, has by his or her actions placed himself or herself entirely beyond the pale of the moral law and, consequently, lost every moral right—including the moral right that fellow citizens respect his or her legal rights. Against moral outlaws, such as those who engage in or promote abortions, any and every form of violence is morally permissible. Thus, antiabortion terrorism, whether it be vigilantism or not, is morally justified when it is directed against moral outlaws.

Perhaps enough has been said to answer the question under consideration. Can one take moral rights seriously and at the same time hold that terrorism is sometimes morally justified? Can one grant the existence of moral rights in the strong sense that renders them incapable of being overridden by a net balance of benefits over harms and, without inconsistency, add that, on rare occasions, terrorism is not morally wrong? I believe that one can. Our examination of antiabortion terrorism in the United States shows that when one considers the rights, or alleged rights, of all parties, the moral rightness or wrongness of such terrorism remains in doubt. It is a mistake to assert that taking rights seriously necessarily rules out any possible justification of terrorism. Whether any act or series of acts of terrorism is morally justified remains an open question.

Pursue the matter further. Taking rights seriously, which includes recognizing the multiplicity of moral rights and the various ways in which they are relevant to any terroristic act, strongly suggests, although it does not prove, that there can be morally justified terrorism. This writer remains firmly convinced that the recent antiabortion bombings in our country are morally wrong. But this is because the presuppositions of those who defend such bombings are not accepted. If the human fetus did have a full right to life, and if bombing so-called abortion clinics were an effective way to prevent or greatly reduce the number of abortions, and if this means of preventing abortions did not indiscriminately destroy very much untainted property or property of the innocent, then it would be morally justified.

One can even dimly see the crucial elements in a plausible justification of such terrorism. It would not be a utilitarian justification that disregards or underestimates moral rights; it would be a rights-based justification. It would ground the right of the terrorists to bomb the clinics upon the more fundamental right—even the duty—to protect the moral rights of the potential victims of those who murder unborn children. It would not deny that the means used to protect moral rights harm, very seriously harm, many victims of the terroristic activity. But precisely because it takes rights seriously, it would not regard these harms as outweighing the right to life of the fetus. It would add that most of the destruction of and damage to property violates no moral property rights because the owners have forfeited their rights by using this property in their immoral activities of murder, inciting to murder, and aiding the physicians engaged in serial murders. Finally, occasional destruction of or damage to untainted property or property of the innocent does not render antiabortion bombings immoral because in this tragic situation the right to property conflicts with the right to life and the right to life of the unborn children overrides the right to property.

This is not suggesting that antiabortion terrorism is morally justified if only it is practiced more responsibly and under different circumstances. Rather, this is a sketch of what would be a rights-based moral justification of this sort of terrorism and might be a model that can be applied to other sorts of terrorism. Still, to see dimly the elements in a plausible justification of terrorism is one thing; to ascertain whether any instance of this model would be a fully adequate justification is quite another. Space limitations do not allow us to complete this second, and more important, task here. But a beginning can be made by discussing, very briefly, some of the theoretical questions raised by the model described.

First, should one take moral rights seriously? That is, should one interpret "a moral right" in Dworkin's strong sense such that the possession of a moral right renders certain ways of treating the right-holder morally wrong even when such mistreatment is useful? I believe that one should, and essentially for the reason that he suggests:

> What he [one who takes rights seriously] cannot do is to say that the Government is justified in overriding a right on the minimum grounds that would be sufficient if no such right existed. He cannot say that the Government is entitled to act on no more than a judgment that its act is likely to produce, overall, a benefit to the community. That admission would make his claim of a right pointless, and would show him to be using some sense of "right" other than the strong sense necessary to give his claim the political importance it is normally taken to have.[8]

Although this argument is far from conclusive, I find it persuasive.

Precisely what this argument shows, and how, may not be obvious to all. Let me therefore, paraphrase what seems to be most revealing in it:

a governmental action that treats any individual adversely, and presumably every governmental action will treat some individuals adversely, requires moral justification. The minimum or weakest ground that would be sufficient to justify such an action is that it would produce a net balance of benefits over harms when its effects on all the members of the community are weighed. If this minimal ground were sufficient to justify an action that not only harmed some individual but also infringed one of his or her moral rights, then the possession of a right would make no moral difference. Since this would deprive moral rights of all importance, if moral rights are to be taken seriously, they cannot be admitted to be overridden by a mere increment in social utility. Although Dworkin's argument is limited to the political rights of the individual holding against the government, its import strikes me as being much more general. If any second party is morally justified in treating a right-holder in a way that infringes any moral right merely because such treatment would be useful, everything considered, then moral rights are unimportant in moral practice and redundant in moral theory. The argument is convincing, therefore, that unless one rejects the existence of moral rights or is willing to concede their triviality, one ought to insist that they cannot be overridden by a mere balance of social utility.

It is not necessary to admit, however, that this requires one to adopt a nonutilitarian theory of the grounds of rights. Dworkin seems to draw precisely this further conclusion. His reasoning goes something like this. If a moral right were grounded in utility, then it could be overridden by utility. But taking rights seriously requires one to deny that moral rights are grounded in utility. He concludes: "anyone who professes to take rights seriously . . . . must accept, at the minimum, one or both of two important ideas. The first is the vague but powerful idea of human dignity. . . . The second is the more familiar idea of political equality." [9] His reasoning is plausible and his conclusion is inviting. Moral rights do not seem to fit comfortably into a utilitarian theory. Nevertheless, it is wiser to decline his invitation to ground moral rights on some nonutilitarian basis such as human dignity or political equality. He concedes that the idea of human dignity is vague. Whether either idea is powerful remains unclear. Both are rhetorically powerful, for both have a persuasive force useful for those who wish to convince their audiences without regard to the truth of their moral or political conclusions. But what we need is logical power, the ability to ground specific conclusions about rights through valid reasoning. And just because these two tempting ideas are so vague, there seems no reasonable way to determine exactly what moral rights, if any, follow from them. A weighing of benefits and harms seems much more promising in this regard. If one could ground moral rights on utility, and this remains to be demonstrated, then it should be possible to replace dogmatic intuitions with an investigation of consequences and to give specific reasons for or against determinate conclusions about rights. Even Dworkin concedes that this might be possible: "he need not consider these ideas to be axiomatic. He may, that is, have reasons for insisting that dignity or equality are important values, and these reasons may be utilitarian." [10]

But how could this be possible? How could one ground rights on social utility, the net balance of benefits over harms when everyone's welfare is considered, without implying that a right can be overridden on this or that occasion by the mere balance of benefits over harms that would result from an act infringing that right? The answer, it seems, lies in the complexity of moral rights. A moral right consists of a complex structure of Hohfeldian elements, especially of moral liberties, claims, powers, and immunities. Presumably, any adequate ground for a moral right must be correspondingly complex. Each of the elements in a specific right will be grounded in utility. Thus a single right will have several distinct utilitarian grounds. Moreover, different kinds of elements will be grounded in utility in different ways. Most crucially, the utilitarian ground of a moral duty will be quite different from the utilitarian ground of a moral power. Therefore, the single utility of an act that would infringe a right will be insufficient to override a right grounded in various ways on several utilities. Or so it seems. It may be that this strategy will evade Dworkin's argument that moral rights must be grounded on some nonutilitarian idea such as human dignity or political equality. Let us pursue this strategy, on a small scale, in the remainder of this essay.

The second theoretical question raised by the model of justification proposed is this: what is the ground of the moral claim-right that others not destroy or damage one's property? Presumably its ground or grounds will reflect its complexity as a structure of Hohfeldian elements. At its core stands the moral claim of the right-holder against others, both other individuals and corporate bodies, that they not destroy or damage one's property. Around this core stand a number of associated elements including (1) the moral power of the right-holder to waive this core claim, (2) the bilateral moral liberty of the right-holder to exercise or refrain from exercising this moral power, and (3) the right-holder's moral immunity against the termination or reduction of his or her core claim by any unilateral act of another. Since each of these elements, and the others included in the complex structure of this right, will have its ground, the grounds of the right as a whole will be complicated indeed. To simplify discussion, let us consider here and now only the grounds of the defining core of this moral right. Although this will save considerable time, it will not eliminate all complexity, for this core claim is itself complex. It consists of the moral duty of others not to destroy or damage one's property together with the moral power of the right-holder to claim performance or remedy in the event of threatened or actual nonperformance of this duty.

At this point, we must confront an awkward question. What could the word "property" mean when one speaks of a moral right that others not destroy or damage one's property? The original and primary meaning of the word "property," according to the *Oxford English Dictionary,* is "the right (*esp.* the exclusive right) to the possession, use, or disposal of anything (usually a tangible material thing)." [11] Now to use the word "property" in defining moral property rights and then to define this word in terms of moral property rights is surely circular definition of the most futile sort. But how can one break out of this linguistic circle? It will not do to define one's property in terms of mere possession, as that which one has in one's hand or under one's immediate control. A pickpocket may have my wallet in his or her possession. Yet it is I, and not the thief, who has the moral right that others, including the pickpocket, not destroy or damage my wallet and its contents. In what sense is the wallet still mine when it is not in my possession? It remains mine because the conventional rules of my society that define the social institution of property allocate to me dominion over the possession, use, and disposal of the wallet. Whatever might be true of the state of nature, within any society moral property rights presuppose conventional rules that provide an institutional definition of property. Thus, the right under examination here is the moral right that others not destroy or damage whatever the social rules of one's society give one the freedom and control to possess, use, and dispose of virtually as one wishes.

The defining core of this right is the moral claim that others not destroy or damage one's property, property as defined by the conventional rules of one's society. This moral claim implies, and is in part constituted by, the moral duty of others not to destroy or damage one's property. Hence, the ground of the right will necessarily contain the ground of this duty. To say that an act is a duty is to say more, or at least something stronger, than to say that one ought to do the act. For example, one could say that one really ought to see the magnificent exhibition of Picasso's work at the Saint Louis Art Museum, but one hardly has a moral duty to do so. Duties are acts that are morally required or obligatory, not merely highly worthwhile or even preferable to the alternatives in the light of the relevant considerations.

The requiredness of duties can best be explained by the fact that their proximate ground is a special sort of practical reason, a dual-aspect reason, which is a reason both for acting in some specific way and for reacting by imposing moral sanctions upon any agent who fails or refuses to act in this way. What, then, is the proximate ground of the moral duty of others not to destroy or damage one's property? It is the fact that the conventional rules of one's society forbid others to destroy or damage, without one's permission, anything that is allocated by society to one for one to possess, use, and dispose of as one wishes. Although the determinate content of the prohibition will vary from society to society, every society will have some set of property rules and every set of property rules will include some such prohibition. And the proximate ground of the moral duty of others not to destroy or damage one's property is the fact that any such act would violate one of the conventional property rules of the society.

But what makes this sociological fact a dual-aspect practical reason? It is the utility of acting in conformity to this property rule together with the utility of acts of imposing moral sanctions upon those who violate this conventional rule. Thus, the ultimate ground of the moral duty not to destroy or damage property is utility, indeed a pair of utilities. Let us examine each of these utilities in turn.

Why is it useful to act in conformity to the conventional rule prohibiting others from destroying or damaging one's property? Let us begin by noticing that what is forbidden is acts that destroy or damage goods, or at least things taken to be goods. Since destruction or damage of goods reduces the valuable things available for human use or enjoyment, there is a utilitarian presumption against any and all acts that destroy or damage property. On a utilitarian theory, what needs explanation is not so much why it is wrong for others to destroy or damage one's property as why it is not wrong for the owner to destroy or damage his or her own property. One utilitarian reason for following the rule at issue here is simply that to violate it is to lessen the supply of goods available for human use.

A second and more important utility of acts following the rule against destroying or damaging the property of another is that this preserves the security of possession of the right-holder. If others are free to destroy or damage one's property at will, then one's possession of those goods allocated to one by the conventional rules of one's society will be precarious; one's possession may end unpredictably at any time. This will interfere with the central purpose of the entire set of property rules in any society, to locate and secure to the owner dominion (freedom and control) over the use of his or her property. This in turn is of immense value to the individual and to society because of the role that property plays in human projects.

Every human project requires the use of goods of one sort or another, and any long-range project will require long-term control over the instrumental goods needed to carry it out to its end. Any act that destroys or damages one's property may interrupt and frustrate one or more of one's ongoing projects and will certainly restrict the projects one will be able to undertake in the future. But why does this matter? Human projects aim at achieving goals that are taken to be worthwhile and in fact usually are productive of value, either because of goods produced or consumptions enjoyed or both. Moreover, it is one's projects that give meaning or significance to one's actions and experiences. This dimension of meaningfulness is what makes the difference between a trivial and an important action or experience and thereby constitutes a crucial aspect of intrinsic value, that from which the value of every good derives. Acts that conform to the conventional rule prohibiting others from destroying or damaging one's property are typically highly useful because they help to provide an essential condition of pursuing one's projects, the secure possession of goods one might use in one's projects. Acts that violate this conventional rule will frequently frustrate projects already undertaken and prevent the undertaking of some new projects. They will also be harmful in more indirect ways. Most major projects are possible only after considerable capital has been accumulated. But where possession is insecure, the motive to save is weakened or even extinguished. Moreover, many projects can be carried out only by hard work. As Hobbes noted, what rational person will bother to raise crops or build a house knowing that he or she may never be able to eat the food or live in the house or sell either and obtain secure possession of the money thus received for them?

Hobbes emphasized the other crucial utilitarian consideration. Acts of others that destroy or damage one's property are obviously against one's own interest and tend to call forth resentment and retaliation. Conflicts over property are one of the most important, if not the most important, sources of social conflict, and conflicts between the members of a society are very harmful to those individuals and to the entire society. Hence, acting in conformity with the conventional rule prohibiting others from destroying or damaging one's property is useful by minimizing conflicts that are harmful to the conflicting parties and to the society disrupted by them. Acts that violate this rule are not only harmful in causing conflict but in engendering fear of future acts of the same kind. They, thereby, motivate those who have property to take precautionary measures against potential acts of destruction or damage. These may take the form of building thick walls, putting bars on windows, or hiring guards. Although these are not harmful in the obvious sense, they are unproductive uses of goods and services and harmful in the way in which any waste of valuable resources is harmful. When precautionary measures take the form of preemptive strikes, however, they cause conflicts just as much as do the actions they are designed to prevent. The conventional property rules of any society are immensely valuable in large measure precisely because they tend to reduce conflicts between individuals and social disruption and to preserve the order and security essential to any society in which economic prosperity and personal happiness are possible.

Do these utilitarian arguments presuppose that every society tends to adopt and retain the most useful set of conventional rules possible under its circumstances? It seems not. Most, almost all, of the value of any set of property rules lies in the way in which they preserve security of possession and prevent conflicts over goods. What is essential is that there be property rules, not the precise content of these rules. A wide range of social institutions of property can serve these functions and possess great utility. What these arguments do presuppose is a much more modest assumption. The specific form that property rules take in one's society must not be so very harmful that following them lacks the utilities I have mentioned or results in having these utilities outweighed by even greater disutilities. Although one can imagine property rules of this sort, it is doubtful that any society would abide by them for long, even if it stumbled into them by accident.

If my account of the grounds of this moral duty is to be adequate, the utility of following each conventional property rule must be paired with the utility of punishing those who disobey the rule. Why is it useful for third parties to impose moral sanctions upon anyone who violates the conventional rule prohibiting others from destroying or damaging one's property? The primary purpose of blaming and otherwise imposing informal penalties upon those who have violated the rule is to deter these individuals, and others, from further violations. Since such violations are harmful by wasting resources, interfering with human projects, and increasing social conflicts, deterrence is useful in preventing these great evils. Enforcing conventional property rules, whatever the specific form these may take in any given society, is especially useful because of the importance of having fixed rules to govern this sphere of social life. In this respect, they are like rules of the road. Although some rules of the road may be better than others, what is essential is that there be rules of the road and that they be widely known and generally followed. Similarly, the central purpose of any set of property rules is to provide stability and security to possession and to avoid or resolve conflicts over the use of resources. Hence, the efficacy of the conventional rule is even more important than its wisdom. Given the scarcity of resources and human covetousness, property rules will be effective only when enforced with sanctions, often legal sanctions but at least moral ones.

The utility of sanctioning those who disobey the conventional rule prohibiting others from destroying or damaging one's property is not exhausted by the deterrent effectiveness of such sanctioning. It has educational value as well. Most narrowly, punishing violators of the conventional rule reaches the young and reminds the not-so-young of the existence and content of the social norm. More broadly, it tends to inculcate the moral and human values presupposed by and implicit in the rule.

Finally, and importantly, imposing sanctions upon the violator strengthens social solidarity and helps to restore ruptured social relations. A property owner normally relies upon the property rules of his or her society, not only by abiding by them himself or herself, but also by acting on the expectation that others will do so as well. Whenever one's property is destroyed or damaged in violation of the conventional rule, others have taken advantage of one. If third parties, other members of one's society, then stand idly by and do nothing, they are in effect abandoning one and leaving him or her to the mercies of the antisocial individual. But to sanction each violator is to take sides with the victim and assure him or her that he or she has not been betrayed by society and that trust in one's fellow members of society is not misplaced. This preservation or restoration of social solidarity has considerable value by nurturing and sustaining the fellow-feeling, trust, and cooperation necessary in any society in which peace and prosperity and happiness can flourish.

This completes my utilitarian account of the grounds of the moral duty of others not to destroy or damage one's property. The proximate ground of this moral duty is the fact that destroying or damaging one's property is prohibited by the conventional rules of one's society. This is a dual-aspect reason, both a reason for doing one's duty and a reason for observers to impose moral sanctions upon those who violate this duty. What makes this a dual-aspect practical reason, and accordingly the ultimate ground of the moral duty, is utility. Acts of obedience to this conventional prohibition are very useful in the ways I have described; and the actions of observers who sanction violations of this rule are also very useful in several ways. Notice that we have already begun to understand why a net balance of benefits over harms of any act infringing the moral right that others not destroy or damage one's property would not suffice to override that right. Although this would negate the utility of following the conventional rule on this particular occasion, it would leave the utility of sanctioning violations of the rule virtually untouched.

There is more to my story, however, because a claim is more than a duty. A moral claim of X against Y consists of a moral duty of Y plus a moral power of X to claim performance or remedy in the event of threatened or actual violation of this duty. Accordingly, the story must continue to explain the ground of this moral power. Since a moral power is very different from a moral duty, its ground must be appropriately different also. Within a utilitarian framework, the ground of a moral power is not the utility of exercising that power but the change in utility affected by its exercise.

To think clearly about this abstract and difficult matter take a concrete example. Imagine that I have on my front lawn near to the street a statue of a darky with grinning face and arm outstretched as though to hold the reins of my visitor's horse. I think my statue rather cute; some militant liberal regards it as crudely racist and morally offensive. When I refuse to remove my darky, he determines to smash it with a hammer or at least paint the face and hands white. Later I confront him just as he is about to destroy or damage my property. Recognizing the futility of reasoning with so obstinate a liberal, I claim performance of his duty to me before a moral judge. Specifically, I turn to a neighbor or some chance bystander and say "Tell him that he ought not to destroy or damage my property." Presumably, I will be expected to plead my case by giving reasons to support the moral judgment for which I am petitioning, and no doubt the second party will be permitted to plead his case also. Let us imagine that in the end the third party finds in favor of me, the claimant as owner, and against the second party. How will my exercise of the power to claim performance of the duty of others not to destroy or damage one's property have changed the relevant utilities—the utility of performing this duty and the utility of sanctioning its nonperformance?

How does claiming performance of this duty change—that is, increase—the utility of following the conventional rule forbidding others to destroy or damage one's property? (1) It normally increases the probability of negative moral sanctions being imposed upon one who violates this rule. Claiming performance before third parties informs them of the threatened violation and, given their judgment in favor of the right-holder, prepares them to intervene against the second party should he or she go on to violate his or her duty to the owner. Since negative sanctions are in and of themselves evils, the greater the prospect of these evils resulting from a violation of a duty, the greater the utility of performing the duty and forestalling these sanctions.

(2) Claiming performance of a duty potentially intensifies and deepens the conflict between the right-holder and the duty-bearer. To destroy or damage one's property is always to fail to respect one's rights and to injure one. But claiming performance of the duty not to do so when such action is threatened changes the meaning of any subsequent violation of this duty. If another insists upon damaging or destroying one's property after one has claimed performance, he or she is not only failing, but refusing to respect one's rights and displaying a new level of antagonism towards one. This in turn almost inevitably calls forth greater resentment from the owner whose property is destroyed or damaged together with intensified resistance and greater efforts to retaliate. Since one of the central utilities upon which the moral duty is grounded is the usefulness of fixed conventional property rules in preventing, or at least minimizing, conflicts within a society, following these rules has extra utility on those occasions when a violation would intensify and deepen the confrontation between the owner and another bent on destruction or damage. Moreover, a very important factor in minimzing future conflicts and limiting the harm of present ones is preserving the conditions conducive to reconciliation between the parties. Reconciliation will be more difficult between an owner who has claimed performance and a second party who has deliberately ignored this act of claiming and proceeded nevertheless to violate his or her duty to the claimant.

(3) The act of claiming not only potentially deepens the conflict; it broadens it also. Whenever others destroy or damage one's property, there is conflict between the owner and the second party who violates

his or her duty to that owner. If the owner claims performance before some third party and this moral judge has rendered judgment for the owner, then any subsequent violation initiates conflict with the moral judge as well as the victim. Accordingly, performing the duty not to destroy or damage one's property becomes more useful after claiming because it avoids the greater harm of the more widespread conflict.

(4) The destruction or damaging of one's property even after one has claimed performance of the duty of others not to do so constitutes a greater threat to property and tends to cause a greater nonproductive expenditure of resources in precautionary measures. One who violates this duty even after the owner has claimed its performance and a moral judge has decided that the contemplated destruction or damage would be morally wrong openly displays an indifference toward the rights of property owners and a disrespect toward the standards of the moral community. Such persons are more dangerous than most, and reasonable individuals will take precautions against their future actions. But the use of economic resources for such nonproductive purposes is harmful in the sense that it is relatively wasteful, unproductive in comparison with the uses for which such resources could be employed. Thus, performing the duty after claiming is more useful than it would be in the absence of the act of claiming because it does not lead to the extra waste that a violation under these circumstances would produce. In at least four ways, then, the act of claiming performance of the moral duty of others not to destroy or damage one's property increases the utility of performing this duty. The grounds of the moral power to claim performance are these changes in utility produced by the exercise of this power.

How does claiming performance of the duty of others not to destroy or damage one's property increase the utility of imposing negative moral sanctions upon those who violate this duty to the right-holder? (1) It increases the deterrent value of these sanctions. The usefulness of punishment as a deterrent depends in considerable measure upon the fact that the action punished was not accidental or out of character and the fact that it provides a clear example to others. The act of claiming puts the second party on notice of the nature of his or her contemplated action, and any subsequent action will be deliberate and voluntary. Again, claiming performance, together with pleading one's case before the moral judge, puts the nature of the act on record, as it were, and makes clear its immoral nature to others, even when the wrongdoer may remain unconvinced. Moreover, to fail to sanction the violation after the right-holder has claimed performance would be to undermine "respect" for the moral law—respect in the limited sense of the general awareness that violations will be met with sanctions.

(2) Although it is generally useful to deter agents from wrongdoing, the imposition of sanctions is also harmful in various ways. Not only are negative moral sanctions undesirable from the standpoint of those upon whom they are applied, often when third parties sanction wrong-doers, they are at the same time intruding into the lives of right-holders who might wish to deal with this conflict in their own way. Such invasions into the private affairs of the victims of wrongdoing are harmful because they are often felt as unwelcome, they may interfere with ongoing projects of the persons wronged, and threaten the personal security so necessary to the full development of individual personality and intimate personal relations. But when the right-holder claims performance by petitioning some third party to intervene, all this is changed. To impose sanctions after the exercise of the power to claim is not to intrude unasked but to respond to an appeal. Therefore, the utility of these acts of punishment will not be reduced by the harms typical of uninvited invasions into the private life of the victim.

(3) The imposition of sanctions is understandably disliked, even resented, by the party who is the object of moral disapproval, condemnation, or other penalties. Even though moral sanctions are short of force, and thus less unwelcome than many legal sanctions, they often alienate the recipient from the punisher, and even the standards upon which the punishment is based. But sanctions are less likely to alienate, or at least alienate radically and permanently, the person upon whom they are imposed if they are imposed only after the right-holder has claimed performance of the duty of others not to destroy or damage one's property. This is because the second party has been given fair warning by this act of claiming, and the moral judge will have punished only after due consideration of the nature of the act and any special circumstances present in this case.

(4) The act of claiming introduces reason into the confrontation between the property owner and the second party threatening to destroy or damage his or her property. One claims performance of a duty by petitioning some third party to serve as moral judge of the dispute. The claimant is expected to plead his or her case by giving reasons in support of the moral judgment for which he or she is suing, and the defendant is presumed to have the right to challenge the reasons given and to counter with reasons to support his or her own case. Thus, the act of

claiming encourages more reasonable thought and action by the parties to the conflict. The greatest danger in most confrontations is that the conflict will get out of hand because the participants overreach themselves or overreact to the threats or injuries they face. Reasonableness is exceedingly useful because it tends to moderate action, limit confrontation, and preserve the conditions necessary for the eventual resolution of the conflict in a way that will reduce the social damage it does. In at least these four ways, then, claiming performance of a moral duty increases the utility of imposing moral sanctions upon anyone who subsequently fails to perform the duty claimed. The moral power to claim performance of the duty of others not to destroy or damage one's property is grounded in the ways in which exercising this power changes, by augmenting, the utility both of performing this duty and imposing negative sanctions upon one who fails to do so.

Consider how these strands of reasoning mesh together. Recall the second theoretical question raised by my model for the justification of terrorism: what is the ground of the moral claim-right that others not destroy or damage one's property? This right, like all moral rights, is grounded on utility. But since this right, again like every right, is a complex of Hohfeldian elements, it must be grounded in a complex set of distinct but related utilities. The core of this moral right is a moral claim of the owner against other parties. This in turn consists of the duty of others not to destroy or damage one's property together with the moral power of the right-holder to claim performance or remedy in the event of threatened or actual nonperformance of this duty by some second party. Since the proximate ground of any duty is some dual-aspect reason, a reason for acting and for reacting, the ultimate ground of this duty must be the utility of refraining from destroying or damaging one's property paired with the utility of imposing negative moral sanctions upon any second party who does not do so. Since a power is very different from a duty, its ground must be appropriately different; it must lie in some change of utility. The ground of the moral power to claim this particular duty is the increase in the utility of performing the duty brought about by the exercise of this power paired with the increase in the utility of imposing moral sanctions upon those who fail to do so brought about by the same exercise of the power. To complete my utilitarian account of this moral right I would have to go on to show how each associated element, such as the power to waive this core claim and the bilateral liberty of exercising or not exercising this power to waive one's claim, can be grounded in utility also.

Space does not permit the completion of my story here, but perhaps enough has been written to make reasonably clear the kind of story that would be told. It is a thoroughly utilitarian story, although quite unlike the familiar forms of act-utilitarianism or rule-utilitarianism. It might well be called a reasons-utilitarianism. A moral right consists of a complex structure of moral positions, such as moral liberties or claims or powers. Since moral positions are positions under moral norms and moral norms consist of moral reasons, the proximate grounds of any moral right are constituted by a set of moral reasons. But these are morally relevant reasons because they are connected with utility and disutility in important ways. Hence, the ultimate grounds of any moral right are utilitarian.

Let us now try to draw some edifying conclusions from all this. Can we conclude that moral rights are, *pace* Dworkin, grounded in utility? Not yet. To do so at this point would be jumping to a conclusion, taking a leap of faith over a series of logical gaps. Before it would be reasonable to draw any such conclusion, we would need to complete my story of the grounds of the claim-right that others not destroy or damage one's property by showing that every one of its associated elements is also grounded in utility. Then we would have to go on to see whether similar stories can be told for other moral rights. Further, we must compare these stories with nonutilitarian stories with regard to factual accuracy and logical relevance. Then we must ascertain whether our utilitarian theory of the grounds of moral rights can be extended to answer the other theoretical questions posed by my model for the justification of terrorism. For example, when and why does the immoral use of one's property forfeit one's moral property rights to the possession so misused? Does the moral right to life override the moral right to property, and if so, why? Do the grounds of moral rights also ground a moral right of third parties to protect those rights? Only after one has shown that these questions, among many, can be answered satisfactorily will one have established a plausible and illuminating theory of the grounds of moral rights.

Can we conclude that terrorism is sometimes morally justified? Not with any confidence. To be sure, a model has been proposed for the justification of terrorism that seems applicable to some exceptional but quite possible cases. But this model raises a number of difficult theoretical questions, and we will not know how these ought to be answered until we have a more complete and adequate theory of rights before us.

What we can conclude, without further ado and with confidence, is that whether terrorism is ever morally justifiable remains an open question. It is not true, or at least we do not yet know it to be true, that taking moral rights seriously necessitates the condemnation of terrorism, no matter what form it takes or under what circumstances it is undertaken. Several moral rights of various parties bear on any act of terrorism, such as the recent antiabortion bombings in our country, and these rights bear on terrorism in a number of distinct ways. Thus, terrorists can appeal to moral rights to justify their acts, just as antiterrorists can appeal to rights to condemn their actions. This is why the question of whether terrorism is ever morally justified will remain an open question until moral philosophers have advanced further their theoretical investigations. No doubt this will disappoint anyone who expects contemporary philosophy to provide a practical solution to the urgent problem of terrorism in our world today. But our modest conclusion may have some practical relevance, for to my mind it suggests a certain tolerance toward the moral convictions and the motives of our moral enemies— those who stand and fight on the other side of fundamental moral issues. This may be at least a small part of the practical answer to the threat of terrorism because intolerance has always been and remains today one of the main sources of terrorism.

NOTES

1. "Florida: More Abortion Bombings."
2. Beck and Greenberg, "The Abortion Clinic Bombings."
3. Magnuson, "Explosions Over Abortion."
4. Universal Declaration of Human Rights, Art. 12.
5. Locke, *Second Treatise of Civil Government,* ch. 2, pp. 5–6.
6. "Florida: More Abortion Bombings."
7. *Wilson v. Atlantic Coast Line R. Co.*
8. Dworkin, *Taking Rights Seriously,* pp. 191–92.
9. Ibid., p. 198.
10. Ibid., p. 199.
11. *Oxford English Dictionary,* vol. 8, p. 1471.

References

Index

References

CASE CITATIONS

Bates v. State Bar of Arizona, 433 U.S. 350 (1977).

Bigelow v. Virginia, 421 U.S. 809 (1975).

Head v. Colloton and Filer, Sup. Ct. Iowa (1983).

Holland v. Metalious, 105 N.H. 290, 198 A.2d 654 (1964).

In Re Richardson, 284 So.2d 185 (La. Ct. App. 1975).

Lausier v. Pescinski, 67 Wis.2d 44, 226 N.W.2d 180 (1975).

Little v. Little, 57766 S.W.2d 493 (Tex. Ct. App. 1979).

McFall v. Shimp, Allegheny County Ct. Common Pleas, 10 Pa. D & C 3d 90 (July 26, 1980).

Strunk v. Strunk, 445 S.W.2d 145 (Ky. 1969).

Wilson v. Atlantic Coast Line R. Co., 55 S.E. 260.

BIBLIOGRAPHY

Ackerman, Terrence F. "What Bioethics Should Be." *Journal of Medicine and Philosophy* 5 (Sept. 1980): 260–75.

Aiken, William, and LaFollette, Hugh, eds. *World Hunger and Moral Obligation*. Englewood Cliffs, N.J.: Prentice-Hall, 1977.

Basson, Marc D., ed. *Ethics, Humanism, and Medicine*. New York: Alan R. Liss, 1980.

———. "Choosing Among Candidates for Scarce Medical Resources." *Journal of Medicine and Philosophy* 4 (Sept. 1979): 313–33.

Bayles, Michael D., ed. *Ethics and Population*. Cambridge, Mass.: Schenkman Publishing Co., 1976.

———. *Morality and Population Policy*. University: Univ. of Alabama Press, 1980.

———. *Professional Ethics*. Belmont, Calif.: Wadsworth Publishing Co., 1981.

Beck, Melinda, and Greenberg, Nikki Finke. "The Abortion Clinic Bombings." *Newsweek* 104 (Dec. 3, 1984): 31.

Berelson, Bernard, and Lieberson, Jonathan. "Government Efforts to Influence Fertility: The Ethical Issues." *Population and Development Review* 5 (Dec. 1979): 581–613.

Bernstein, Dorothy M. "The Organ Donor." *Journal of the American Medical Association* 237 (1977): 2643–44.

Bernstein, Dorothy M., and Simmons, Roberta G. "The Adolescent Kidney Donor: The Right to Give." *American Journal of Psychiatry* 131 (Dec. 1974): 1338–43.

Bok, Sissela. *Lying: Moral Choice in Public and Private Life*. New York: Pantheon Books, 1978.

Bondeson, William B., et al., eds. *New Knowledge in the Biomedical Sciences: Implications of its Acquisition, Possession, and Use*. Dordrecht: D. Reidel, 1982.

Brandt, Richard B. *A Theory of the Good and the Right*. Oxford: Clarendon Press, 1979.

Burt, Robert A. "Coercion and Communal Morality." *Journal of Health Politics, Policy and Law* 9 (Summer 1984): 323–24.

Cabot, Richard. *Honesty*. New York: Macmillan, 1938.

Callender, Clive O.; Bayton, James A.; Yeager, Curtis; and Clark, John E. "Attitudes Among Blacks Toward Donating Kidneys for Transplantation: A Pilot Project." *Journal of the National Medical Association* 74 (1982): 807–9.

Caplan, Arthur L. "Ethical Engineers Need Not Apply: The State of Applied Ethics Today." *Science, Technology and Human Values* 6 (1980): 24–32.

———. "Organ Procurement: It's Not in the Cards." *Hastings Center Report* 14 (Oct. 1984): 9–12.

Caplan, Arthur L.; Lidz, Charles W.; Meisel, Alan; Roth, Loren H.; and Zimmerman, David, "Mrs. X and the Bone Marrow Transplant." *Hastings Center Report* 13 (June 1983): 17–19.

Childress, J. F. "The Gift of Life: Ethical Problems and Policies in Obtaining and Distributing Organs for Transplantation." *Critical Care Clinics* 2 (Jan. 1986): 133–48.

————. "The Implications of Major Western Religious Traditions for Policies Regarding Human Biological Materials." Prepared for the Office of Technology Assessment, May 1986.

————. "Rationing of Medical Treatment." *Encyclopedia of Bioethics,* edited by Warren T. Reich. New York: Macmillan, Free Press, 1978. Vol. 4, pp. 1414–18.

————. "Rights to Health Care in a Democratic Society." *Biomedical Ethics Reviews, 1984,* edited by James M. Humber and Robert F. Almeder. Clifton, N.J.: Humana Press, 1984.

————. "Triage in Neonatal Intensive Care: The Limitations of a Metaphor." *Virginia Law Review* 69 (1983): 547–61.

————. "Who Shall Live When Not All Can Live?" *Soundings* 53 (Winter 1970): 339–55.

Council on Scientific Affairs. "Organ Donor Recruitment." *Journal of the American Medical Association* 246 (1981): 2157–58.

Daniels, Norman. *Just Health Care.* New York: Cambridge Univ. Press, 1985.

Davis, John W.; Hoffmaster, Barry; and Shorten, Sarah, eds. *Contemporary Issues in Biomedical Ethics.* Clifton, N.J.: Humana Press, 1978.

Denise, S. H. "Regulating the Sale of Human Organs." *Virginia Law Review* 71 (1985): 1015–38.

Dewey, John. *Human Nature and Conduct.* New York: Modern Library, 1922.

————. *Middle Works,* vol. 3. Edited by Jo Ann Boydston. Carbondale: Southern Ill. Univ. Press, 1977.

Dickens, Bernard M. "The Control of Living Body Materials." *University of Toronto Law Journal* 27 (Summer 1977): 142–98.

Drucker, Peter F. "Ethical Chic." *Forbes* 14 (Sept. 1981): 160–62, 164–66, 170, 172–73.

————. "What is 'Business Ethics'?" *The Public Interest* 63 (Spring 1981): 18–36.

Dworkin, Ronald M. *Taking Rights Seriously.* Cambridge, Mass.: Harvard Univ. Press, 1977.

Eisendrath, Robert M.; Guttmann, Ronald D.; and Murray, Joseph E. "Psychologic Considerations in the Selection of Kidney Transplant Donors." *Surg. Gynecol. Obstet.* 129 (Aug. 1969): 243–48.

Ethical, Legal and Policy Issues Pertaining to Solid Organ Procurement. A Report of the Project on Organ Transplantation, The Hastings Center (Oct. 1985).

Evans, Roger W.; Blagg, Christopher R.; and Bryan, Fred A., Jr. "Implications for Health Care Policy: A Social and Demographic Profile of Hemodialysis Patients in the United States." *Journal of the American Medical Association* 245 (Feb. 6, 1981): 487–91.

Evans, Roger W. (Project Director and Principal Investigator); and Garrison, Louis P.; Jonsen, Albert R.; Manninen, Diane L.; Overcast, Thomas D.; Junichi, Yagi (Co-investigators). *The National Heart Transplantation Study: Final Report,* vols. 1–5. Seattle: Battelle Human Affairs Research Centers, 1984.

Fellner, Carl H., and Marshall, John R. "Kidney Donors: The Myth of Informed Consent." *American Journal of Psychiatry* 126 (Mar. 1970): 1245–51.

"Florida: More Abortion Bombings." *Newsweek* 105 (Jan. 7, 1985): 17.

Fost, Norman. "Children as Renal Donors." *New England Journal of Medicine* 296 (1977): 363–67.

Fox, Renee C., and Swazey, Judith P. *The Courage to Fail* 2nd ed. Chicago: Univ. of Chicago Press, 1978.

Fuller, Lon L. "Positivism and Fidelity to Law—A Reply to Professor Hart." *Harvard Law Review* 71 (1958): 630–72.

Gewirth, Alan. *Reason and Morality.* Chicago: Univ. of Chicago Press, 1978.

Hare, Richard M. "Abortion and the Golden Rule." *Philosophy and Public Affairs* 4 (Spring 1975): 201–22.

Hart, Herbert Lionel Adolphus. *The Concept of Law.* Oxford: Clarendon Press, 1961.

———. "Positivism and the Separation of Law and Morals." *Harvard Law Review* 71 (Feb. 1958): 593–629.

Hartmann, Nicolai. *Ethics.* 2 vols. New York: Macmillan, 1932.

"The Hastings Center: Ethics in the 80s." *Hastings Center Report* 11 (Dec. 1981), Special Insert.

Health Insurance Association of America. *Organ Transplants and Their Implications for the Health Insurance Industry.* 1985.

Heermance, Edgar L. *Codes of Ethics: A Handbook.* Burlington, Vt.: Free Press Printing Co., 1924.

Hollenberg, Norman K. "Altruism and Coercion: Should Children Serve As Renal Donors?" *New England Journal of Medicine* 296 (1977): 390–91.

Humber, James M. and Almeder, Robert F., eds. *Biomedical Ethics Reviews, 1984.* Clifton, N.J.: Humana Press, 1984.

Kant, Immanuel. *Kant's Critique of Practical Reason and Other Works on the Theory of Ethics.* Trans. T. K. Abbott. London: Longmans, Green, 1879.

———. *The Moral Law: Kant's Groundwork of the Metaphysics of Morals.* Trans. by H. J. Paton. New York: Barnes & Noble, 1963.

Katz, Jay, and Capron, Alexander Morgan. *Catastrophic Disease: Who Decides What?* New York: Russell Sage Foundation, 1975.

Kaufman, H. H.; Huchton, J. D.; McBride, M. M.; Beardsley, C. A., and

Cahan, B. D. "Kidney Donation: Needs and Possibilities," *Neurosurgery* 5 (Aug. 1979): 237–44.

Knox, Richard A. "Heart Transplants: To Pay or Not to Pay?" *Science* 209 (Aug. 1, 1980): 570–75.

Ladd, John. *The Structure of a Moral Code.* Cambridge, Mass.: Harvard Univ. Press, 1957.

Lansing, Paul. "The Conflict of Patient Privacy and The Freedom of Information Act." *Journal of Health Politics, Policy and Law* 9 (Summer 1984): 315–22.

Levey, Andrew S.; Hou, Susan; and Bush, Harry L., Jr. "Kidney Transplantation from Unrelated Living Donors: Time to Reclaim a Discarded Opportunity." *New England Journal of Medicine* 314 (Apr. 3, 1986): 914–16.

Lieberson, Jonathan. Book Review of Michael D. Bayles, *Morality and Population Policy,* in *Population and Development Review* 7 (Mar. 1981): 119–31.

Liebling, J. A., ed. *The Republic of Silence.* New York: Harcourt, 1947.

Locke, John. *The Second Treatise of Civil Government and A Letter Concerning Toleration.* Edited by J. W. Gough. Oxford: Basil Blackwell, 1946.

Magnuson, Ed. "Explosions Over Abortion." *Time* 125 (Jan. 14, 1985): 17.

Manninen, Diane L., and Evans, Roger W. "Public Attitudes and Behavior Regarding Organ Donation." *Journal of the American Medical Association* 253 (June 7, 1985): 3111–15.

Mauss, Marcel. *The Gift.* Trans. of *Essai sur le don* (1925) by Ian Cunnison. New York: Norton, 1967. (Glencoe, Ill.: Free Press, 1954.)

May, William F. "Religious Justifications for Donating Body Parts," *Hastings Center Report* 15 (Feb. 1985): 38–42.

Meisel, Alan, and Roth, Loren H. "Must a Man Be His Cousin's Keeper?" *Hastings Center Report* 8 (Oct. 1978): 5–6.

"Most in U.S. Found Willing to Donate Organs." *New York Times,* Jan. 17, 1968, p. 18, col. 4.

Muyskens, James L. "An Alternative Policy for Obtaining Cadaver Organs for Transplantation." *Philosophy and Public Affairs* 8 (Fall 1978): 88–99.

National Organ Transplant Act: Hearings on H.R. 4080 Before The Subcommittee on Health and Environment of the House Committee on Energy and Commerce, 98th Cong., 1st Sess., 1983.

Noble, Cheryl N. "Ethics and Experts." *Hastings Center Report* 12 (June 1982): 7–9.

———. "Response." *Hastings Center Report* 12 (June 1982): 15.

Office of Organ Transplantation. *Organ Transplantation Background Information.* Feb. 11, 1985.

Oh, H. K., and Uniewski, M. H. "Enhancing Organ Recovery by Initiation of Required Request Within a Major Medical Center." *Transplantation Proceedings* 18, no. 3 (June 1986): 426–28.

Oldenquist, Andrew. "Rules and Consequences." *Mind* 75 (Apr. 1966): 180–92.

Parsons, V., and Lock, P. "Triage and The Patient With Renal Failure." *Journal of Medical Ethics* 6 (Dec. 1980): 173–76.

Pence, Gregory E. *Ethical Options in Medicine.* Oradell, N.J.: Medical Economics, 1980.

Perry, Clifton. "Human Organs and The Open Market." *Ethics* 91 (Oct. 1980): 63–71.

Powledge, Tabitha M., and Fletcher, John. "Guidelines for the Ethical, Social and Legal Issues in Prenatal Diagnosis." *New England Journal of Medicine* 300 (1979): 168–72.

President's Commission for the Study of Ethical Problems in Medicine and Biomedical and Behavioral Research. *Securing Access to Health Care.* Vol. 1: Report (Mar. 1983).

Prottas, Jeffrey. "Encouraging Altruism: Public Attitudes and the Marketing of Organ Donation." *Milbank Memorial Fund Quarterly/Health and Society* 63 (Winter 1985): 278–306.

———. "Organ Procurement in Europe and the United States." *Milbank Memorial Fund Quarterly/Health and Society* 63 (Winter 1985): 94–126.

Ramsey, Paul. *The Patient as Person.* New Haven: Yale Univ. Press, 1970.

Rawls, John. *A Theory of Justice.* Cambridge: Harvard Univ. Press, 1971.

Redfield, Robert. *The Primitive World and Its Transformations.* Ithaca: Cornell Univ. Press, 1953.

"Regulating the Sale of Human Organs," Note. *Virginia Law Review* 71 (Sept. 1985): 1015–38.

Report of the Massachusetts Task Force on Organ Transplantation. Presented to the Commissioner of Public Health and Secretary of Human Services, Massachusetts (Oct. 1984).

Rescher, Nicholas. "The Allocation of Exotic Medical Lifesaving Therapy," *Ethics* 79 (Apr. 1969): 173–86.

Robertson, John A. "Organ Donations by Incompetents and the Substitute Judgment Doctrine." *Columbia Law Review* 76 (Jan.1976): 48–78.

Rosner, Fred, and Bleich, J. David, eds. *Jewish Bioethics.* New York: Sanhedrin Press, 1979.

Rubin, Joe. "Malpractice Board Urged by MD/Lawyer." *Medical Post* 1 (Dec. 1981): 17.

Schneider, A., and Flaherty, M. P. "Woman Passed Over." *Pittsburgh Press,* Sun., May 12, 1985.

Schwartz, Howard S. "Bioethical and Legal Considerations in Increasing the Supply of Transplantable Organs: From UAGA to 'Baby Fae.'" *American Journal of Law and Medicine* 10 (Winter 1985): 397–437.

Shue, Henry. "Exporting Hazards." *Ethics* 91 (July 1981): 579–606.

Simmons, A. John. "Tacit Consent and Political Obligation." *Philosophy and Public Affairs* 5 (Spring 1976): 274–95.

Simmons, R., and Klein, S. *Gift of Life: The Social and Psychological Impact of Organ Transplantation.* New York: John Wiley, 1977.

Starzl, Thomas E. "Will Live Organ Donations No Longer Be Justified?" *Hastings Center Report* 15 (Apr. 1985): 5.

Steinbrook, Robert L. "Kidneys for Transplantation." *Journal of Health Politics, Policy and Law* 6 (Fall 1981): 504–19.

Stevenson, Charles L. *Ethics and Language.* New Haven: Yale Univ. Press, 1944.

Stiller, C. R.; McKenzie, F. N.; and Jostuk, W. J. "Cardiac Transplantation: Ethical and Economic Issues." *Transplantation Today* 2 (Feb. 1985): 22–25.

Stuart, Frank P.; Veith, Frank J.; and Cranford, Ronald E. "Brain Death Laws and Patterns of Consent to Remove Organs for Transplantation from Cadavers in the United States and 28 Other Countries." *Transplantation* 31 (1981): 238–44.

Task Force on Organ Transplantation. Final Report. *Organ Transplantation: Issues and Recommendations.* Washington, D.C.: U.S. Dept. of Health and Human Services, Government Printing Office, Apr. 1986.

Task Force on Organ Transplantation. *Report to the Secretary and the Congress on Immunosuppressive Therapies.* Washington, D.C.: U.S. Dept. of Health and Human Services, Government Printing Office, Oct. 1985.

Titmuss, Richard. *The Gift Relationship.* New York: Pantheon, 1971.

Uniform Anatomical Gift Act (1968).

Universal Declaration of Human Rights (1948).

The U.S. Public's Attitudes Toward Transplants/Organ Donation, A Gallup Survey, The Gallup Organizations, Jan. 1985.

Veatch, Robert M., ed. *Values and Life-extending Technologies.* New York: Harper & Row, 1979.

———. "Voluntary Risks to Health: The Ethical Issues." *Journal of the American Medical Association* 243 (Jan. 4, 1980): 50–55.

Wikler, Daniel. "Ethicists, Critics and Expertise." *Hastings Center Report* 12 (June 1982): 12.

Winslow, Gerald R. *Triage and Justice: The Ethics of Rationing Life-saving Medical Resources.* Berkeley: Univ. of California Press, 1982.

Wing, Antony J. "Why Don't the British Treat More Patients with Kidney Failure?" *British Medical Journal* 287 (Oct. 22, 1983): 1157–58.

Wokutch, Richard E., and Carson, Thomas L. "The Ethics and Profitability of Bluffing in Business." *Westminster Institute Review*, May 1981, pp. 7–9.

Index

165

John Howie, Professor of Philosophy at Southern Illinois University, Carbondale, received his Ph.D. degree from Boston University. He is the author of *Perspectives for Moral Decisions*, editor of *Ethical Principles for Social Policy*, and coeditor of *Contemporary Studies in Philosophical Idealism* and *The Wisdom of William Ernest Hocking*, and has published articles in *The Philosophical Forum*, *Stylus*, *Educational Theory*, *The Calcutta Review*, *Darshana International*, *Idealistic Studies*, *Religious Studies*, *Bulletin of Bibliography and Magazine Notes*, and *Indian Philosophical Quarterly*.